Bronson Alcott's Fruitlands

Compiled by Clara Endicott Sears with Transcendental Wild Oats

By Louisa M. Alcott

Published by Pantianos Classics

ISBN-13: 978-1-78987-540-9

First published in 1876

This edition is based upon a reprint of 1915

The Old House at Fruitlands, Harvard, Massachusetts

In front are the mulberry trees planted by the philosophers for the propagation of silkworms

Contents

Note v
Foreword v
Introduction vi

Bronson Alcott's Fruitlands 9

   I - A New Eden 9

   II - The Founding of Fruitlands 19

   III - Brook Farm and Fruitlands 25

   IV - The Man with the Beard 34

   V - Summer Sunshine 41

   VI - Father Hecker's Description of Fruitlands 45

   VII - Anna Alcott's Diary at Fruitlands, 1843 50

   VIII - Louisa May Alcott's Diary at Fruitlands 61

   IX - Autumn Disappointment 64

   X - In After Years 74

   XI - Transcendental Wild Oats 82

Appendix 96

Note

I Desire to express my thanks to Mr. John S. Pratt Alcott, of Brookline; Mr. F. B. Sanborn, of Concord; Dr. Joseph Wiswall Palmer, of Fitchburg; and Mr. Alvin Holman, of Leominster, for facts and data concerning the Consociate Family at Fruitlands, and for their assistance in collecting and acquiring the greater part of the original furniture which was there in the days of the Community.

And I further thank Mr. John S. Pratt Alcott for the privilege of including Louisa's and Anna's Diaries at Fruitlands, and Mr. Alcott and Messrs. Little, Brown & Company for the use of Louisa M. Alcott's *Transcendental Wild Oats*.

Clara Endicott Sears.

Foreword

For many years articles have appeared from time to time in magazines and books regarding the Community at Fruitlands, but it has remained for Miss Sears to gather them together with infinite patience for publication, and this little book is the result, the first connected story of the life and beliefs of that little Community which tried so hard to live according to its ideals in spite of criticism and censure and whose members nearly starved as a result of their devotion.

A great deal of credit is due to Miss Sears for her success in gathering material to make this story of Fruitlands so complete, and I take this opportunity, as the oldest surviving member of the Alcott family, of expressing to her our gratitude for the very interesting and complete account of the Fruitlands experiment.

John S. P. Alcott.

Introduction

Longfellow wrote: —

"All houses wherein men have lived and died
Are haunted houses. Through the open doors
The harmless phantoms on their errands glide,
With feet that make no sound upon the floors.

"We meet them at the doorway, on the stair,
Along the passages they come and go,
Impalpable impressions on the air,
A sense of something moving to and fro.

"We have no title-deeds to house or lands;
Owners and occupants of earlier dates
From graves forgotten stretch their dusty hands.
And hold in mortmain still their old estates.

"The spirit world around this world of sense
Floats like an atmosphere, and everywhere
Wafts through these earthly mists and vapors dense
A vital breath of more ethereal air."

I found myself reciting these lines whenever my eyes rested upon the old house of Fruitlands. From my terrace on the hill I looked down upon it with mixed feelings of pity, awe, and affection. It seemed like a Presence, a ghost of the Past, that compelled the eyes to gaze at it persistently. In the warm joyousness of the spring sunshine, or when the cold mists of autumn crept across the valley, it conveyed to me the same sense of desolation, of mystery, of disillusionment. Its broken windows looked like hollow eyes sunken in an ashen and expressionless face. Within its walls life and death had come and gone; — laughter and the sound of weeping had echoed through the quaint, low-ceilinged rooms. It had been the sheltering home of British yeomen. Its heavy chestnut beams bore record of the virgin forests of the Colonies. The thrill of patriotism had vibrated there when the sword of the Revolution swept the land, and the sound of drum and fife, leading the hurrying feet of eager volunteers to Concord and Lexington, must have reached the quiet hillside and stirred the hearts of those listening in the doorway. Those were the brave and vital days of its youth. In seed-time and harvest it had smiled upon the valley, its shingles warm and ruddy with ochre-red. At Yule-tide the log had been chosen with fitting ceremony and placed within the broad and spacious chimney. The old and the young had feasted and made merry to the sound of the crackling fire-music. Who can tell what memories of happiness and romance the old house contains?

Then came a period of quiet years, when the meadows and pastures grew rich and fertile, the upturned soil yielded abundant harvests, and the branches of the apple trees hung heavy with fruit. But it was when the old house had begun to settle and look decrepid, and its floors had become shaky and uneven, that its door opened wide to its supreme experience. Then Fruitlands was exalted into the New Eden. The two names came to it simultaneously. It was to pulsate with lofty ideals and altruistic aspirations. For one perfect summer and mellow autumn its running brook, its shady grove, its fertile meadows and sloping pasture, its western view, so beautiful at sundown, of Wachusett and Monadnoc, and the chain of purple hills, were to be the inspiration of a group of individuals then known as the transcendental philosophers, and through them Fruitlands became famous. Within its walls great questions were discussed, great hopes for the betterment and enlightenment of mankind were generated. Alcott, Charles Lane, Wright, Bower, Emerson, Hawthorne, Channing, Thoreau, and many others went in and out of its doors; and last, but not least, the child, Louisa May Alcott, who later became our well-loved New England authoress, and Joseph Palmer, a Crusader in spirit as well as in actions, who suffered for his principle of wearing a beard at a time when it was looked upon as a badge of scorn and contempt, and which won for him the name of "the Old Jew." When the beautiful dream was over; when the New Eden proved to be only an empty mockery of the vision it had once inspired; when the great experience had ended in failure, then the old house sagged pitifully as if its heart had broken: the winter storms and summer rains of the succeeding years washed all color from its face: it became gray and haggard. Joseph Palmer and his wife lingered on in old age, and then passed out into the Beyond. Their children and grandchildren clung to the place for a space of years, but its history was over. It was left desolate and abandoned.

So as I looked down on it from my terrace on the hill, pitying its infinite loneliness, the thought came to me that I must save it. If for a time it had borne the semblance of a New Eden, then that time must be honored, and not forgotten. I longed to see it smiling again upon the valley in its glowing coat of ochre-red. The fine old chimneys must be put back in their places from which they had been ruthlessly torn down to make room for stoves. The hollow eyes must gleam again with window-panes; the sound of voices must ring once more through the empty rooms. In the future it must be cherished for its quaintly interesting history. If that history was full of pathos, if the great experiment enacted beneath its roof proved a failure, the failure was only in the means of expression and not in the ideal which inspired it. Humanity must ever reach out towards a New Eden. Succeeding generations smile at the crude attempts, and forthwith make their own blunders, but each attempt, however seemingly unsuccessful, must of necessity contain a germ of spiritual beauty which will bear fruit. Let no one cross the threshold of the old house with a mocking heart. Looking back from our present coigne of vantage, we, too, cannot but smile at the childlike simplicity and credulity, and the lack of forethought of those unpractical enthusiasts. But let it be the smile of tenderness and not of derision. In this material age we cannot afford to lose any details of so unique and picturesque a memory as that of A. Bronson Alcott and the "Con-Sociate Family" at Fruitlands.

Bronson Alcott's Fruitlands

I - A New Eden

The following account of the Fruitlands Community is largely a compilation of writings regarding it by eye-witnesses and those in close touch with its members. This is the surest way of forming a just estimate of the experiment and the characters involved.

Mr. Frank B. Sanborn, in his book entitled "Bronson Alcott," describes in a few short sentences the circumstances which led up to the formation of the Community, and this is what he says: —

"James Pierrepont Greaves was an Englishman born in 1777, who at the age of forty went to reside in Switzerland with Pestalozzi, for four years, and there adopted, a few years before young Alcott did, the chief ideas of Pestalozzi, as to the training of children. Returning to England in 1825, he gradually formed a circle of mystics and reformers, in London and its vicinity, who were, like himself, interested in the early instruction and training of children. Hearing from Harriet Martineau, upon her return from America in 1837, of Mr. Alcott's Temple School at Boston, and thinking more favorably of it than Miss Martineau did, Mr. Greaves opened a correspondence with the American Pestalozzi, and received from him some of his books, — Miss Peabody's 'Records of a School,' and Mr. Alcott's 'Conversations on the Gospels.' From these books, and from his correspondence, Mr. Greaves and his friends, William Oldham, Mrs. Chichester, Charles Lane, Heraud, and others, formed so high an estimate of Bronson Alcott's talents and character, that they named for him the English school they were about establishing near London, and called it 'Alcott House.' They also urged Mr. Alcott to visit them in England and to take part in their schemes and labors. He was well inclined to do this; and in 1842 he set sail for London, where, late in May, he received a hearty welcome from his correspondents and their circle, with the exception of Mr. Greaves, who had died earlier in the same year."

Mr. Emerson furnished the money for Mr. Alcott's trip to England. The following letter was written by Bronson Alcott to his cousin Dr. William Alcott:

Alcott House,
Ham Common, Surrey,
June 30, 1842.

...I am now at Alcott House, which is ten miles from London; where I find the principles of human culture, which have so long interested me, carried into practical operation by wise and devoted friends of education. The school

ABIGAIL MAY, MRS. A. BRONSON ALCOTT
From a daguerreotype

A. BRONSON ALCOTT AT THE AGE OF 53
From the portrait by Mrs. Hildreth

was opened five years ago and has been thus far quite successful. It consists of thirty or more children, and some of them not more than three years of age, — all fed and lodged at the House. The strictest temperance is observed in diet and regimen. Plain bread with vegetables and fruits is their food, and water their only drink. They bathe always before their morning lesson, and have exercises in the play-grounds, which are ample, besides cultivating the gardens of the institution. They seem very happy and not less in the schoolroom than elsewhere.

Mr. Wright has more genius for teaching than any person I have before seen — his method and temper are admirable, and all parties, from assistants, of which there are several, to the youngest child delight in his presence and influence. He impersonates and realizes my own idea of an education, and is the first person whom I have met that has entered into this divine art of inspiring the human clay, and moulding it into the stature and image of divinity. I am already knit to him by more than human ties, and must take him with me to America, as a coadjutor in our high vocation, or else remain with him here. But I hope to effect the first.

- - - - -

The Healthian is edited here by Mr. Wright and Mr. Lane, and they contribute to almost every reform journal in the kingdom. They are not ignorant of our labors in the United States, almost every work of any value I find in the library at Alcott House, — your own works, those of Mr. Graham (a vegetarian), besides foreign authors not to be found with us. I shall bring with me many books, both ancient and modern, on my return to America.

It was during his sojourn in England in 1842 that the idea of creating "a New Eden," as he loved to call it, took firm root in Alcott's mind. A more quaintly unique character than his cannot be found in all the annals of our literary history. His unquenchable aspirations after the ideal life caught the imagination of men and women ready to break away from the narrowing tendency of the Orthodox faith of the time. He was both loved and derided. A transcendentalist pure and simple; unpractical; a dreamer and visionary in every sense of the word; yet his mind emitted flashes of genius so unerring and decisive as to elicit the spontaneous admiration of Ralph Waldo Emerson and impel him to write in his journal the following tributes: —

"The comfort of Alcott's mind is, the connection in which he sees whatever he sees. He is never dazzled by a spot of colour, or a gleam of light, to value the thing by itself; but forever and ever is prepossessed by the individual one behind it and all. I do not know where to find in men or books a mind so valuable to faith in others.

"For every opinion or sentence of Alcott a reason may be sought and found, not in his will or fancy, but in the necessity of Nature itself, which has daguerred that fatal impression on his susceptible soul. He is as good as a lens or a mirror, a beautiful susceptibility, every impression on which is not to be reasoned against, or derided, but to be accounted for, and until accounted for, registered as an indisputable addition to our catalogue of natural facts. There are defects in the lens, and errors of retraction and position, etc., to be allowed for, and it needs one acquainted with the lens by frequent use, to make these allowances; but 't is the best instrument I have met with." [1]

"Once more for Alcott it is to be said that he is sincerely and necessarily engaged to his task and not wilfully or ostentatiously or peculiarily. Mr. Johnson at Manchester said of him, 'He is universally competent. Whatever question is asked, he is prepared for.'

"I shall go far and see many, before I find such an extraordinary insight as Alcott's. In his fine talk last evening, he ran up and down the scale of powers with much ease and precision as a squirrel the wires of his cage, and is never dazzled by his means, or by any particular, and a fine heroic action or a poetic passage would make no impression on him, because he expects heroism and poetry in all. Ideal Purity, the poet, the artist, the man must have. I have never seen any person who so fortifies the believer, so confutes the skeptic. And the almost uniform rejection of this man by men of parts, Carlyle and Browning inclusive, and by women of piety, might make one despair of society. If he came with a cannonade of acclaim from all nations, as the first wit on the planet, these masters would sustain the reputation; or if they could find him in a book a thousand years old, with a legend of miracles appended, there would be churches of disciples; but now they wish to know if his coat is out at the elbows, or whether somebody did not hear from somebody, that he has got a new hat etc. He has faults, no doubt, but I may safely know more about them than he does; and some that are most severely imputed to him are only the omissions of a preoccupied mind." [1]

"Last night in the conversation Alcott appeared to great advantage, and I saw again, as often before, his singular superiority. As pure intellect I have never seen his equal. The people with whom he talks do not ever understand him. They interrupt him with clamorous dissent, or what they think verbal endorsement of what they fancy he may have been saying, or with 'Do you know Mr. Alcott I think thus and so,' — some whim or sentimentalism, and do not know that they have interrupted his large and progressive statement; do not know that all they have in their baby brains is incoherent and spotty; that all he sees and says is like astronomy, lying there real and vast, every part and fact in eternal connection with the whole, and that they ought to sit in silent gratitude, eager only to hear more, to hear the whole, and not interrupt him with their prattle. It is because his sight is so clear, commanding the whole ground, and he perfectly gifted to state adequately what he sees, that he does not lose his temper when glib interlocutors bore him with their dead texts and phrases. — Power is not pettish, but want of power is." [2]

"Yesterday Alcott left me after three days spent here. I had laid down a man and had waked up a bruise, by reason of a bad cold, and was lumpish, tardy and cold. Yet I could see plainly that I conversed with the most extraordinary man and the highest genius of the time. He is a man. He is erect; he sees, let whoever be overthrown or parasitic or blind. Life he would have and enact, and not nestle into any cast-off shell or form of the old time, and now proposes to preach to the people, or to take his staff and walk through the country, conversing with the school-teachers, and holding conversations in the villages. And so he ought to go, publishing through the land his gospel like them of old time." [3]

The Small Entry Where the Valuable Books Were Kept

It was not unnatural that these gifts, fully acknowledged by so eminent a man as Emerson, should have won to him the respect and devotion of these

Englishmen, who were living in the same atmosphere of thought in which Bronson Alcott lived and moved and had his being. And so after much discussion and many plans, illumined by great hopes and a deep enthusiasm, Charles Lane and Mr. Alcott collected a valuable library of books mostly on mysticism and all occult subjects for the future Eden, and with William Lane, who was Charles Lane's son, Wright, and Samuel Bowers, sailed for America, their immediate destination being the home in Concord where Mrs. Alcott and her daughters, then very young, were waiting to receive them.

Concord named the strangers "the English Mystics" and received them cordially into the inner circle of literary men which formed the group now spoken of as the "Concord Philosophers." Emerson, Thoreau, Hawthorne, Ellery Channing, and others became their friends, and listened to their plans for forming universal brotherhood. Emerson's description of Charles Lane was this: —

"A man of fine intellectual nature, inspired and hallowed by a profound faith. This is no man of letters, but a man of ideas. Deep opens below deep in his thought, and for the solution of each new problem, he recurs, with new success to the highest truth, to that which is most generous, most simple, and most powerful; to that which cannot be comprehended, or overseen, or exhausted. His words come to us like the voices of home out of a far country."

In the mean time the trunks containing the books chosen in England with so much care were opened, and lists were made of their contents. It was either Emerson or Thoreau who inserted a notice of them in "The Dial," the famous periodical to which the literary men and women of this noted circle contributed. It ran thus: "Mr. Alcott and Mr. Lane have recently brought from England a small, but valuable library, amounting to about 1000 volumes, containing undoubtedly a richer collection of mystical writers than any other library in this country. To the select library of the late J. P. Greaves, 'held by Mr. Lane in trust for universal ends,' they have added many works of a like character, by purchase or received as gifts. In their Catalogue...they say, 'The titles of these books are now submitted, in the expectation that this Library is the commencement of an Institution for the nurture of men in universal freedom of action, thought, and being. We print this list, not only because our respect is engaged to views so liberal, but because the arrival of this cabinet of mystic and theosophic lore is a remarkable fact in our literary history.'"

Mr. Sanborn, referring to this library in his "Bronson Alcott," says: "It was this collection which, in the summer of 1843, occupied a hundred feet of shelving in the old red farmhouse at Fruitlands."

The problem of where to establish the New Eden became the great and vital question of the moment. Many suggestions were offered from many quarters, but the great impediment to a definite decision was the lack of funds. Mr. Alcott had no money to spare to put into a farm such as they required, and the group of friends were interested, but not wholly convinced of the feasibility of the scheme, and hung back when it came to a question of investment. This very doubt fanned the flame of desire in Mr. Alcott and Charles Lane to prove to the world the value of their cherished dream. So it came about that Charles Lane took the burden of paying for a farm on his own shoulders, and he wrote the following letter to Mr. Alcott's brother, Junius Alcott, on March 7, 1843: —

"I hope the little cash I have collected from my London toils will suffice to redeem a small spot on the planet, that we may rightly use for the right owner. I would very much prefer a small example of true life to a large society in false and selfish harmony. Please put your best worldly thoughts to the subject and favor me with your view as to how and where we could best lay out $1800 or $2000 in land, with orchard, wood, and house. Some of the land must be now fit for the spade, as we desire to give all animals their freedom. We feel it desirable to keep within the range of Mind and Letters; or rather to keep refinement within our range, that we may be the means of improving or reproving it, without being injured by it."

Before this Mr. Alcott had written a letter to Isaac T. Hecker, later known as Father Hecker, head of the Paulist Brotherhood, and in it he described the idea they had in mind. At that time Father Hecker was at Brook Farm, but was restless and dissatisfied with the life there, craving a more ascetic existence; and knowing this, Alcott felt confident of his sympathy and stated the salient points of the scheme to him: —

Our purposes, as far as we know them at present, are briefly these: —

First, to obtain the free use of a spot of land adequate by our own labor to our support; including, of course, a convenient plain house, and offices, wood-lot, garden, and orchard.

Secondly, to live independently of foreign aids by being sufficiently elevated to procure all articles for subsistence in the productions of the spot, under a regimen of healthful labor and recreation; with benignity toward all creatures, human and inferior; with beauty and refinement in all economics; and the purest charity throughout our demeanor.

Should this kind of life attract parties toward us — individuals of like aims and issues — that state of being itself determines the law of association; and the particular mode may be spoken of more definitely as individual cases may arise; but in no case, could inferior ends compromise the principles laid down.

Doubtless such a household, with our library, our services and manner of life, may attract young men and women, possibly also families with children, desirous of access to the channels and fountains of wisdom and purity; and we are not without hope that Providence will use us progressively for beneficial effects in the great work of human regeneration, and the restoration of the highest life on earth.

With the humane wish that yourself and little ones may be led to confide in providential Love, I am, dear friend,

Very truly yours,

A. Bronson Alcott.

February 15, 1843.

Finally a decision was arrived at, and in a letter to Mr. Oldham, Charles Lane narrates how it came about. It was written from Concord, May 31, 1843:

My dear Friend: —
...Mr. Alcott and I walked up the river to a place called the Cliffs, where is a young orchard of 16 acres and woodland below. He came home with his head full of poetic schemes for a cottage, etc., on this spot. I, however, came home first and found that a man had been sent by the young man who walked with me to Southborough, having a farm to sell at Harvard, 14 miles off. He proposed to take me directly to see it, but I was fatigued, so Samuel Larned, the visitor who came up with Mr. Wright, went in the waiting vehicle. The next morning being very fine Mr. Alcott and I walked there, not knowing his name, but we ascertained it to be Wyman; we saw his place, consisting of 90 acres, 14 of them wood, a few apple and other fruit trees, plenty of nuts and berries, much of the land very good; the prospect from the highest part very sublime. The house and barn very poor, but the water excellent and plentiful. The capabilities are manifold, but the actualities humble. For the whole he asked 2700 dollars, which being beyond my means, we had much talk when he offered to sell the land for 1800 dollars and to lend us the buildings gratis for a year. I should observe it is extremely retired, there being no road to it. On these terms we have closed. He gives us the few crops he has just planted and grass to a considerable amount will soon be cut. I have slept a night or two there. William and two friends (Larned and Abram Everett, called the "Plain Man" in the *Vermont Telegraph*) and a hired man remain there, and the family are to start early tomorrow morning, so now for plenty of work of all sorts. Ninety acres; much of it first rate; some worth 100 dollars per acre, the whole 20 dollars per acre; would that some of the English honest half-starved were on it! This, I think you will admit, looks like an attempt at something which will entitle transcendentalism to some respect for its practicality...We have very much to do, but the occasions are opportune. I think Mr. Emerson is not so well pleased with our departure as he would be with our company, but as he did nothing to keep us we must go. It appeared to me that for the hopefulness of many, it was needful we should make a movement of some kind this year, even though we fail; and Providence seems really to have worked for us...

I thank you very much for the £10; the note arrived very opportunely to enable Mr. A. to quit Concord, to do which all his debts must be paid, and I need not tell you on whom that falls. Our transactions at present leave me about 500 dollars in debt, but every one says we have made a good bargain in the purchase of the land. I seriously hope we are forming the basis for something really progressive, call it family or community, or what you will...

We have now plenty of work to do and how we get on I shall faithfully report, though the pen will not do much at present...

Believe me, dear friend,

Yours steadfastly in the spirit,

Charles Lane.

Mr. Sanborn, who above all others has an intimate knowledge of what the situation was, having in later years learned much concerning it from Emerson and Alcott and others of that time, makes this comment in his "Bronson Alcott": —

"After looking at several places in Concord and elsewhere. Lane decided to buy the Wyman farm at Harvard, two miles from the village of that name, but less than a mile from Still River, another village in the same township. Alcott would have chosen the Cliffs in Concord, a favorite resort of Thoreau and the Emerson family, and Emerson would have preferred to retain his friend in his own town; but Lane had rather avoided Emerson, as not ascetic enough for his abstemious habits, and seems to have been not unwilling to withdraw Alcott from what he regarded as an unfavorable influence."

But when it was all settled, Alcott and his English Mystics entered into their plan with a touching enthusiasm. Before them lay vistas of glowing possibilities. They dreamed dreams and saw visions of a "Peace on Earth, Good Will towards Men" such as had never before been realized. There was much to be done and they were eager to begin, — the days were none too long in which to collect the necessary things before moving to Harvard. So Charles Lane persuaded Samuel Bowers to write to Oldham a description of the farm, he himself being too busy to do so. And Bowers writes as follows: —

"Charles Lane wished me to sketch to you the material picture of Fruitlands and the adjoining scene, but I am unqualified to do justice to the subject. The property is very compact and may be a very beautiful domain. It is part a hill sloping down to more valley. Several springs gush out from the side of the hill and the water is very good — better I think than is common in Massachusetts. The soil varies much, but the average quality is, I considerately judge, twice, if not thrice as good as that of Tytherley. [4] There is about 14 acres of woodland all in the vale and adjoining is the Nashua River, on the other side of which, where the receding lands gently rise, stands a Shaker village (Shirley), its extended orchards, corn and grass lands. There is in view a long and high range of hills, one of which, and that the highest, is famous for having been the resort of an Indian sachem. The hill is called Wachusett. Altogether the scene reminded me strongly of the Vale of Evesham, in Worcestershire, where seen when one approaches it from Oxford."

It is quite evident that Oldham had written a letter to Charles Lane warning him against assuming too great responsibility in this venture. The question as to whether many enthusiasts would join the Community was a very crucial one, since it was on this expectation that they based their plans of running the farm free of debt. In answering the letter he asks Oldham to forward certain money due to him. And in his explanation says: —

"I do not see any one to act the money part but myself." (This refers to the land for the Fruitlands experiment.) "Mr. Alcott cannot part with me. I deem him too sincere and valuable to quit him, and besides there is nothing in the country so well as we can show if we be faithful; but rents, debts, and mortgage would destroy us. As to the recruits you speak of, are they good for anything? Are they worth the small passage money you name? Truly if they are some of them you have at Alcott House, I think we should not be much aided by their presence.

"Understand, we are not going to open a hospital. We are more Pythagorean than Christs, we wish to begin with the sound rather than to heal the sick. There is grand work here to be done and I must not trifle with it."

This matter of getting the right kind of persons to join the Community required a keen insight into human nature, and on this point Mr. Alcott was not very strong. His own sincerity and depth of purpose were so great that he looked for these same attributes in every one who approached him, and often failed to detect the superficial qualities that lurked underneath the surface enthusiasm of some of his followers. At this time Transcendentalism was rife through the land. Some called it "the Newness." The expression "Apostles of the Newness" was heard on all sides. They could be recognized by their long hair, Byronic collars, flowing ties, and eccentric habits and manners. Nothing seemed too excessive to prove their emancipation from the shackles of conventionality. One day three young men of this kind turned up at Mr. Emerson's at Concord and entered into an animated conversation with him on his front porch. With them freedom of thought and allegiance to "the Newness" took the strange form of preceding every remark, however trivial, with resounding oaths, which so startled the passers-by, and Mr. Emerson as well, that he hastily invited them to move round to the back of the house where the vibrations of their sulphurous ejaculations might roll harmlessly across the meadow instead of exploding in through the windows of the houses near by.

That Mr. Emerson was deeply interested in the experiment of creating the "New Eden" at Harvard is shown by the fact that a deed of the land was made out in his name as trustee for Charles Lane. He and Thoreau and the rest of the Concord circle viewed the departure with a mixture of interest, curiosity, and anxiety. On June 10, 1843, Emerson wrote to Thoreau: —

"From Mr. Alcott and Mr. Lane at Harvard, we have yet heard nothing. They went away in good spirits, having sent Wood Abram and Larned and William Lane before them, with horse and plough, a few days in advance, to begin the spring work. Mr. Lane paid me a long visit, in which he was more than I had ever known him gentle and open; and it was impossible not to sympathize with and honor projects that so often seem without feet or hands."

[1] Emerson's *Journal*, 1856.

[2] Emerson's *Journal,* 1856.
[3] Emerson's Journal, 1857.
[4] The location of Owen's Harmony Hall in England.

II - The Founding of Fruitlands

The original members of the Community that started the unique experiment were Mr. Alcott, his wife, and four small daughters, the Englishman Charles Lane and his son William, H. C. Wright (for a short time) and Samuel Bower, Isaac T. Hecker, of New York, Christopher Greene and Samuel Larned, of Providence, Abraham Everett and Anna Page, Joseph Palmer, of Fitchburg, and Abram Wood. The transcendentalism of this last individual showed itself chiefly in insisting upon twisting his name hind side before and calling himself "Wood Abram." As this he was always known at Fruitlands. These members did not all arrive at once, but came within a short time of each other. Wright had shown some dissatisfaction already in the extreme asceticism of the plan of life adopted by Mr. Alcott at Concord and he refused to be a regular member of the Fruitlands Community on this account. In writing to Oldham on the subject Charles Lane says: "I can see no other reason but the simplicity and order to which affairs were coming (in the cottage); no butter nor milk, nor cocoa, nor tea, nor coffee. Nothing but fruit, grain, and water was hard for the inside; then regular hours and places, cleaning up scraps, etc., was desperate hard for the outside."

When finally the move from Concord to Harvard was made, Mr. Alcott took what furniture he could with him, such as beds, etc., and the rest was supplied by Joseph Palmer, who carted his over from his old Homestead at No Town outside of Fitchburg.

Shortly after the move, Charles Lane sat down and wrote to Thoreau a description of Fruitlands:

Fruitlands, June 7, 1843.

It is very remotely placed, without a road, surrounded by a beautiful green landscape of fields and woods, with the distance filled up with some of the loftiest mountains in the State. At present there is much hard manual labor, so much that, as you see, my usual handwriting is very greatly suspended. Our house accommodations are poor and scanty; but the greatest want is good female society. Far too much labor devolves on Mrs. Alcott. Besides the occupations of each succeeding day, we form in this ample theatre of hope, many forthcoming scenes. The nearer little copse is designed as the site of the cottages. Fountains can be made to descend from their granite sources on the hill-slope to every apartment if desired. Gardens are to displace the warm grazing glades on the South, and numerous human beings instead of cattle, shall here enjoy existence.

On the estate are about 14 acres of wood, — a very sylvan realization, which only wants a Thoreau's mind to elevate it to classic beauty. The farther wood offers to the naturalist and the poet an exhaustless haunt; and a short cleaning up of the brook would connect our boat with the Nashua. Such are the designs which Mr. Alcott and I have just sketched, as resting from planting we walked around this reserve.

Though to me our mode of life is luxurious in the highest degree, yet generally it seems to be thought that the setting aside of all impure diet, dirty habits, idle thoughts, and selfish feelings is a source of self-denial scarcely to be encountered, or even thought of, in such an alluring world as this.

In the course of the next few weeks Lane wrote with much detail to Oldham: —

Fruitlands, Harvard, Mass.,
June 16, 1843.

My dear Friend: —

The morning being rainy I have taken advantage of the suspension of outdoor labours to sit down and have a little chat with you of and concerning our doings and progress. The day after I wrote you last all the household effects and all the household were mounted on wheels and trundled to this place; the old little cottage being left as clean as a new book by Mrs. Alcott's great energy. The day was sharp and cold for the season, but the weather has since come out fine and warm, some days hot. We have all been busily engaged in manual operations in the field, house, wood yard, etc. Planting, ploughing, sowing, cleaning fruit trees, gardening, chopping, sawing, fitting up, etc., etc., have gone at a rapid rate, as the place was in a very slovenly condition. When tired we have taken a look round the estate to see what was growing, learn the shape of it, and its capabilities with more minuteness. It seems to be agreed on all hands, and we have opinions from many practical men, that we have not made a bad exchange, even in the commercial sense, of our cash for land. Only think, brother Oldham, ninety acres, every one of which may, in a short time, and without much outlay, be brought into a state fit for spade culture; and much of it very good land, obtained at the rate of 20 dollars or only *four pounds per acre freehold*. Recollect, too, this includes fuel and some building material, for there are 14 acres of wood, including many trees of edible nuts, and still only 30 miles from a metropolitan city of 110,000 inhabitants. [1] The land is most beautifully disposed in hill and valley, and the scenery is of a sublime and elevating character. Water abundant and excellent and the springs being on the hill, it may be conveyed anywhere about the place for irrigation, etc. As is common in this district, the principal part is meadow and pasture; but we shall go on ploughing up as much as possible, sowing crops of clover or buckwheat, and turning them in, so as to redeem the land without animal manures, which in practice I find to be as filthy as in idea. The use of them is disgusting in the extreme. At present, we have about 4 acres in Maize, 1½ in Rye, 1½ in Oats, 1 in Barley, 2 in Potatoes, nearly 1 in Beans, Peas, Melons, Squashes, etc.; there will be some Buckwheat, Turnips, etc., making in all about 11 acres arable. We have no Wheat this year. The grass promises well, and we may possibly cut 200 dollars' worth; but by hired teams we are now turning up one piece of 8 or 9, and another of 5 acres, and mean to attack another 4 or 5 for our next year's homestead or garden, should we obtain the means of building. The hillside of 12 or 14 acres pasture is also to be ploughed, directly, if we can; so that the work of reclamation will go rapidly forward. There is a large piece of peat land, as black as ink, which, mixed with sand, makes a most productive soil, valued at 200 to 300 dollars per acre; and there is sand on our lot within 100 yards. We have been much plagued, and a little cheated, with the cattle, but our stock is now reduced to one yoke of oxen.

Besides Mr. Alcott, his Wife and Children, myself and William, who is very efficient and active, we have only a Mr. Lamed and Abraham [Abram Everett] — who appears in the *Vermont Telegraph* as the "Plain Man." Larned was many months at West Roxbury, is only about 20 years of age, his father was a merchant, and he has been a counting-house man and is what the world calls genteel. Abraham is about 42, a cooper by trade, but an excellent assistant here, very faithful to every work he undertakes, very serious, has had rather deep experience, having been imprisoned in a mad house by his relations because he had a little property, but still he is not a spiritual being, at least not consciously and wishfully so.

I have exchanged more letters with Samuel Bower and he promises to come here to-morrow. If his real state bears out his writings, I think he may be added to the family, otherwise he thinks of looking at Roxbury for the purpose of finding a home there...

Mr. Alcott is as persevering in practice as last year we found him to be in idea. To do better and better, to *be* better and better, is the constant theme. His hand is everywhere like his mind. He has held the plough with great efficiency, sometimes for the whole day, and by the straightness of his furrow may be said to be giving lessons to the professed ploughmen, who work in a slovenly manner. We have called in the aid of a carpenter who has made simple shelves for our books, and for the first time our library stands upright as it should do. It occupies about 100 feet of shelves.

June 28, 1843.

On the 19th I received your very kind and newsful letter of the first instant enclosed in Mrs. Chichester's. Mr. Bower, having kept his promise, was here, and I read much of it at breakfast, having also another visitor from Brook Farm, Mr. Hecker [Isaac T. Hecker]. All were much interested in the facts reported, and Saml. Bower heard your remembrances fresh from your pen. You affect him more than any other person. In your next, you will perhaps devote a slip to him and I will forward it. He, Lamed and Hecker visited the Shakers and were much attracted by them. Larned who, on common report, used to oppose them, talks of joining them, so pleasant is their society; at least at first...

The Study
A bust of Socrates stands on the fine old Dutch highboy that Joseph Palmer brought from No Town

If I were not at this moment surrounded by so much that is beautiful in the present, hopeful in the future and ennobling in the act, your affectionate invitation to Ham would seriously touch me. But by God's blessing something shall be done here which shall reach you there. *If we can aid the people in any way to let self be conquered, we shall do something.* Lust abounds and love is deserted. Lust of money, of food, of sexuality, of books, of music, of art, — while Love demands the powers devoted to these false ends. I thank you for your hint respecting worldliness. I believe I am getting on safe ground if I am not already landed. From, or in England you say, I should expect nothing, and I am now in the same predicament here. Every farthing I had is now either put in or involved in this affair, and more, for I have put my hand to two rather large bills; silly enough, you will say. In a few weeks I expect to be literally pennyless, and even unable for want of stage hire to travel to Boston if you send me ever so many orders, of which you discover I have been so neglectful. No; I think I am now out of the money world. Let my privation be ever so great, I will never make any property claim on this effort. It is an offering to the Eternal Spirit, and I consider that I have no more right than any other person; and I have arranged the title deeds, as well as I could, to meet that end. I could only consent to return to England on condition of being held free, like a child, from all money entanglements. As no person or association can guarantee this for me, I think it would be better to remain here where the simple wants can be so easily met, and where there is much opportunity for doing good, and more hope as the outward conditions are so beautifully free. Would that you were here for a month; we have now the most delightful steady weather you can conceive; we are all dressed in our linen tunics, Abraham is ploughing, Larned bringing some turf from the house, Alcott doing a thousand things. Bower and I have well dug a sandy spot for carrots, the children and Lady are busy in their respective ways, and some hirelings are assisting...Now that something, though little, is doing, you will find my expressions more peaceful. Con-fi-dence in Love I hope will ne'er be wanting in your affectionate friend,

Charles Lane.

Fruitlands, Harvard, Mass.,
July 30, 1843.

Dear Friend: —

...A few days after I wrote you Samuel Bower joined us and has steadily and zealously entered into all the works and speculations we have in hand and mind. Mr. Hecker, a very spiritual-minded young man, also has been with us. He is partner with his brothers at New York in a very extensive baking and corn mill business. He has resided several months at W. Roxbury, but is by no means satisfied with their schoolboy dilettante spiritualism. He will, I believe, go to New York to clear up if possible with his family as to the relations on which they are in future to stand to each other. They appear to be so loving and united a family with such strong human attachments that, although he has done much towards breaking away, I fear that in the desire to bring his brothers further into the inner world, he will himself be detained.

Mr. Alcott and I returned last evening from a short visit to Boston to purchase a few articles, and while there we went out one evening to Roxbury [2] where there are 80 or 90 persons playing away their youth and daytime in a miserably joyous, frivolous manner. There are not above four or five who could be selected as really and truly progressing beings. Most of the adults are there to pass "a good time"; the children are taught languages, etc.; the animals (in consequence I believe solely of Mr. George Ripley's tendency) occupy a prominent position, there being no less than 16 cows, besides 4 oxen, a herd of swine, a horse or two, etc. The milk is sold in Boston, and they buy butter to the extent of 500 dollars a year. We had a pleasant summer evening conversation with many of them, but it is only in a few individuals that anything deeper than ordinary is to be found. The Northampton Community is one of industry, the one at Hopedale aims at practical theology, this of Roxbury is one of taste; yet it is the best which exists here, and perhaps we shall have to say it is the best which can exist. At all events we can go no further than to keep open fields, and as far as we have it open house to *all* comers. We know very well that if they come not in the right name and nature they will not long remain. Our dietetic system is a test quite sufficient for many. As far as acres of fine land are concerned, you may offer their free use to any free souls who will come here and work them, and any aid we can afford shall be freely given. The aid of sympathetic companionship is not small, and that at least we can render. To bridge the Atlantic is a trifle if the heart is really set on the attainment of better conditions. Here are they freely presented, at a day's walk from the shore, without a long and expensive journey to the West. Please to advertise these facts to all youthful men and women; for such are much wanted here. There is now a certain opportunity for planting a love colony, the influence of which may be felt for many generations, and more than felt; it may be the beginning for a state of things which shall far transcend itself. They to whom our work seems not good enough may come and set out a better.

I should mention to you that passing his door Mr. Theodore Parker came to the Community in the evening and again in the morning. He is a very popular man at present and has a congregation at Roxbury, but being unwell by reason of close study, he will sail to Europe on the 1st September. He will remain in Germany for three or four months, and afterwards as long in England. No doubt you will see him and render him all the service you can...At present we are not sought by many persons, but the value in our enterprise depends not upon numbers so much as upon the spirit from which we can live outwardly and in all relations true to the intuitions which are gifted to us. We must not forget how great have been the works done by individuals, and in the absence of what are usually called facilities. Our obstacles are, I suppose, chiefly within, and as these are subdued we shall triumph in externalities. I could send you a description of works and crops, our mowing, hoeing, reaping, ploughing in tall crops of clover and grass for next year's manure, and various other operations, but although they have some degree of relation to the grand principle to which they are obedient, they are worth little in the exoteric sense alone. Perhaps the external revelations of success ought always to be kept secret, for every improvement discovered is only turned to a money making account and to the further degradation of man, as we see in the march of science to this very moment. If we knew how to double the crops of the earth, it is scarcely to be hoped that any good would come by revealing the mode. On the contrary, the bounties of God are already made the means by which man debases himself more and more. We will therefore say little concerning the sources of external wealth until man is himself secured to the End which rightly uses these means...

Mr. Charles Stearns Wheeler, the eminent Greek student, who went from here to Germany last summer, died at Leipsic [3] in June, age 26. He was one of Mr. Emerson's great hopes.

Samuel Bower continues with us, but he is not so happy in body or mind as he ought to be: a letter from you in the universal spirit would cheer him up. He confesses to the possession of a little Nomadic blood in his veins. He thinks Mr. Alcott is arbitrary or despotic, as some others do, but I shall endeavour (and, I think, not in vain) to urge him to the noblest conduct of which our position is capable. He must not complain nor walk off, but cheerfully amend whatever is amiss. I suppose your letter has failed at the post somewhere, but I have inquired fully on this side. With assurances of continued affection to yourself and all friends on the divine ground,

I remain, dear Oldham,

Truly yours,

Charles Lane

[1] Boston.
[2] Brook Farm.
[3] This should be Rome.

III - Brook Farm and Fruitlands

There is so much confusion in the minds of many regarding the difference of aim existing in the Community at Brook Farm and that of Fruitlands that it seems well to insert here a well-authenticated account of Brook Farm and also an extract from a letter written by John Sullivan Dwight who was a member.

Brook Farm was a Community established in West Roxbury, Massachusetts, in 1841. "The head of the Community was George Ripley, formerly a Unitarian clergyman in Boston, who had been in 1836 one of the Founders of the Transcendental Club with Emerson, Hedge, Alcott, and others. Associated with Ripley in the Brook Farm enterprise were Nathaniel Hawthorne, Charles A. Dana, John S. Dwight, and other well-known men. They bought a farm comprising some 200 acres. Its object was the establishment of an 'agricultural, literary, and scientific school or college.'

"Several trades beside agriculture were carried on and a number of children were received as pupils, instruction being furnished in ancient and modern languages, history, mathematics, moral philosophy, music, drawing, etc. It was designed to substitute cooperative for selfish competition, and to dignify bodily labor by uniting it with the intellectual and spiritual life. The Community was at first organized as a joint-stock company, each subscriber being guaranteed 5 per cent per annum on his shares. In 1847 the experiment, having proved a failure financially, was given up.

"Life at Brook Farm, especially during the first years of enthusiasm, had idyllic and romantic aspects. In its palmiest state the Community, including school children and boarders, numbered about 150 souls. Kitchen and table were in common; very little help was hired, but philosophers, clergymen, and poets worked at the humblest tasks, milking cows, pitching manure, cleaning stables, etc., while cultivated women cooked, washed, ironed, and waited on table. All work, manual or intellectual, was credited to members at a uniform rate of ten cents an hour."

John Sullivan Dwight wrote of Brook Farm: —

"I remember the night of my first arrival at Brook Farm. It had been going all summer. I arrived in November. At that time it was a sort of pastoral life, rather romantic, although so much hard labor was involved in it. They were all at tea in the old building, which was called the Hive. In a long room at a long table they were making tea, and I sat down with them. When tea was over they were all very merry, full of life; and all turned to and washed the dishes, cups and saucers. All joined in, — the Curtis brothers, Dana and all. It was very enchanting, quite a lark, as we say. Much of the industry went on in that way, because it combined the freest sociability with the useful arts."

Robert Carter, a co-editor with James Russell Lowell of a magazine called *The Pioneer* in 1843, wrote an article called "The Newness" in after years, describing Fruitlands and Brook Farm. Of the latter he says: —

"It was a delightful gathering of men and women of superior cultivation, who led a charming life for a few years, laboring in its fields and philandering in its pleasant woods. It was little too much of a picnic for serious profit, and the young men and maidens were rather unduly addicted to moonlight wanderings in the pine grove, though it is creditable to the sound moral training of New England that little or no harm came of these wanderings — at least, not to the maidens. Brook Farm, however, was not the only Community which was founded by the disciples of the 'Newness.' There was one established in 1843 on a farm called Fruitlands, in the town of Harvard, about forty miles from Boston. This was of much more ultra and grotesque character than Brook Farm. Here were gathered the men and women who based their hopes of reforming the world and of making all things new on dress and on diet. They revived the Pythagorean, the Essenian, and the Monkish notions of

Asceticism with some variations and improvements peculiarly American. The head of the institution was Bronson Alcott, a very remarkable man, whose singularities of character, conduct, and opinion would alone afford sufficient topics for a long lecture. His friend Emerson defined him to be a philosopher devoted to the science of education, and declared that he had singular gifts for awakening contemplation and aspiration in simple and in cultivated persons...His writings, though quaint and thoughtful, are clumsy compared with his conversation, which has been pronounced by the best judges to have been unrivalled in grace and clearness. Mr. Alcott was one of the most foremost leaders of the 'Newness.' He swung round the circle of schemes very rapidly, and after going through a great variety of phases he maintained, at the time of the foundation of 'Fruitlands,' that the evils of life were not so much social or political as personal, and that a personal reform only could eradicate them; that self-denial was the road to eternal life, and that property was an evil, and animal food of all kinds an abomination. No animal substance, neither flesh, fish, butter, cheese, eggs, nor milk, was allowed to be used at 'Fruitlands.' They were all denounced as pollution, and as tending to corrupt the body, and through that the soul. Tea and coffee, molasses and rice, were also proscribed, — the last two as foreign luxuries, — and only water was used as a beverage.

"Mr. Alcott would not allow the land to be manured, which he regarded as a base and corrupting and unjust mode of forcing nature. He made also a distinction between vegetables which aspired or grew into the air, as wheat, apples, and other fruits, and the base products which grew downwards into the earth, such as potatoes, [1] beets, radishes, and the like. These latter he would not allow to be used. The bread of the Community he himself made of unbolted flour, and sought to render it palatable by forming the loaves into the shapes of animals and other pleasant images. He was very strict, rather despotic in his rule of the Community, and some of the members have told me they were nearly starved to death there; nay, absolutely would have perished with hunger if they had not furtively gone among the surrounding farmers and begged for food.

"One of the Fruitlanders took it into his head that clothes were an impediment to spiritual growth, and that the light of day was equally pernicious. He accordingly secluded himself in his room in a state of nature during the day, and only went out at night for exercise, with a single white cotton garment reaching from his neck to his knees.

"Samuel Larned lived one whole year on crackers, and the next year exclusively on apples. He went to Brook Farm after the collapse of the Fruitlands Community, and when that also failed he went South, married a lady who owned a number of slaves, and settled there as a Unitarian minister."

In this same article Mr. Carter asserts that Fourierism brought Brook Farm into disrepute at the end, and that a large wooden phalanstery, in which members had invested all their means, took fire and burned to the ground just as it was completed. Upon this catastrophe the association scattered in 1847. Nathaniel Hawthorne lost all his savings in the enterprise. While he was at Brook Farm he looked after the pigsties.

In contrast to this is the full account of the object and aim of Fruitlands. The following letter on The Consociate Family Life was written to A. Brooke of Oakland, Ohio, and published in the *Herald of Freedom,* September 8, 1843:-

Dear Sir: Having perused your several letters in the *Herald of Freedom,* and finding, moreover, a general invitation to correspondence from "persons who feel prepared to cooperate in the work of reform upon principles" akin to those you have set forth, I take this public means of communicating with one, who seems to be really desirous of aiding entire human regeneration.

After many years passed in admiration of a better order in human society, with a constant expectation that some beginning would shortly be made, and a continued reliance that some party would make it, the idea has gradually gained possession of my mind, that it is not right thus to linger for the leadings of other men, but that each should at once proceed to live out the proposed life to the utmost possible extent. Assured that the most potent hindrances to goodness abide in the Soul itself; next in the body; thirdly in the house and family; and in the fourth degree only in our neighbors, or in society at large; I have daily found less and less reason to complain of public institutions, or of the dilatoriness of reformers of genetic minds.

Animated by pure reform principles, or rather by pure creative spirit, I have not hesitated to withdraw as far and as fast as hopeful prudence dictated from the practices and principles of the Old World, and acting upon the conviction that whatever others might do, or leave undone, however others might fail in the realization of their ideal good, I, at least, should advance, I have accordingly arrived in that region where I perceive you theoretically, and I hope, actually dwell. I agree with you that it would be well to cross the ocean of Life from the narrow island of selfishness to the broad continent of universal Love at one dash; but the winds are not always propitious, and steam is only a recent invention. I cannot yet boast of a year's emancipation from old England. One free step leads to another; and the third must necessarily precede the fourth, as the second was before the third.

A. Bronson Alcott's visit to England last year opened to me some of the superior conditions for a pure life which this country offers compared to the land of my nativity and that of your ancestors. My love for purity and goodness was sufficiently strong it seems to loosen me from a position as regards pecuniary income, affectionate friends, and mental liberty, which millions there and thousands here might envy. It has happened however that of the many persons with whom Mr. Alcott hoped to act in conjunction and concert, not one is yet fully liberated by Providence to that end. So that instead of forming items in a large enterprise, we are left to be the principal actors in promoting an idea less in extent, but greater in intent, than any yet presented to our observation.

Charles Lane

Our removal to this estate in humble confidence has drawn to us several practical coadjutors, and opened many inquiries by letter for a statement of our principles and modes of life. We cannot perhaps turn our replies to better account, than to transcribe some portions of them for your information, and we trust, for your sincere satisfaction.

You must be aware, however, that written words cannot do much towards the elucidation of principles comprehending all human relationships, and claiming an origin profound as man's inmost consciousness of the ever present Living Spirit. A dwelling together, a concert in soul, and a consorting in body, is a position needful to entire understanding, which we hope at no distant day to attain with yourself and many other sincere friends. We have not yet drawn out any preordained plan of daily operations, as we are impressed with the conviction that by a faithful reliance on the Spirit which actuates us, we are sure of attaining to clear revelations of daily practical duties as they are to be daily done by us. When the Spirit of Love and Wisdom abounds, literal forms are needless, irksome or hinderative; where the Spirit is lacking, no preconceived rules can compensate.

To us it appears not so much that improved circumstances are to meliorate mankind, as that I improved men will originate the superior condition for themselves and others. Upon the Human Will, and not upon circumstances, as some philosophers assert, rests the function, power and duty, of generating a better social state. The human beings in whom the Eternal Spirit has ascended from low animal delights or mere human affections, to a state of spiritual chastity and intuition, are in themselves a divine atmosphere, they are superior circumstances and are constant in endeavoring to create, as well as to modify, all other conditions, so that these also shall more and more conduce to the like consciousness in others.

Hence our perseverance in efforts to attain simplicity in diet, plain garments, pure bathing, unsullied dwellings, open conduct, gentle behavior, kindly sympathies, serene minds. These, and several other particulars needful to the true end of man's residence on earth, may be designated the Family Life. Our Happiness, though not the direct object in human energy, may be accepted as the conformation of rectitude, and this is not otherwise attainable than in the Holy Family. The Family in its highest, divinest sense is therefore our true position, our sacred earthly destiny. It comprehends every divine, every human relation consistent with universal good, and all others it rejects, as it disdains all animal sensualities.

The evils of life are not so much social, or political, as personal, and a personal reform only can eradicate them.

Let the Family, furthermore, be viewed as the home of pure social affections, the school of expanding intelligence, the sphere of unbought art, the scene of joyous employment, and we feel in that single sentiment, a fulness of action, of life, of being, which no scientific social contrivance can ensure, nor selfish accident supply.

Family is not dependent upon numbers, nor upon skill, nor riches, but upon union in and with that spirit which alone can bless any enterprise whatever.

On this topic of Family association, it will not involve an entire agreement with the Shakers to say they are at least entitled to deeper consideration than they yet appear to have secured. There are many important acts in their career worthy of observation. It is perhaps most striking that the only really successful extensive Community of interest, spiritual and secular, in modern times was established by A Woman. Again, we witness in this people the bringing together of the two sexes in a new relation, or rather with a new idea of the old relation. This has led to results more harmonic than anyone seriously believes attainable for the human race, either in isolation or association, so long as divided, conflicting family arrangements are permitted. The great secular success of the Shakers; their order, cleanliness, intelligence and serenity are so eminent, that it is worthy of enquiry how far these are attributal to an adherence to their peculiar doctrine.

As to Property, we discover not its just disposal either in individual or social tenures, but in its entire absorption into the New Spirit, which ever gives and never grasps.

While we write, negotiations are entertained for our removal to a place of less inconvenience, by friends who have long waited for some proof of a determination to act up to the idea they have cherished. Many, no doubt, are yet unprepared "to give up all and follow him" (the Spirit) who can importantly aid in the New Advent, and conscientiously accomplish the legal processes needful under the present circumstances. We do not recognize the purchase of land; but its redemption from the debasing state of *proprium,* or property, to divine uses, we clearly understand when those whom the world esteems as owners are found yielding their individual rights to the Supreme Owner. Looking at the subject practically in relation to a climate in which a costly shelter is necessary, and where a family with many children has to be provided for, the possibility of at once stepping boldly out of the toils into which the errors of our predecessors have cast us, is not so evident as it is desirable.

Trade we hope entirely to avoid at an early day. As a nursery for many evil propensities it is almost universally felt to be a most undesirable course. Such needful articles as we cannot yet raise by our own hand labor from the soil, thus redeemed from human ownership, we shall endeavor to obtain by friendly exchanges, and, as nearly as possible, without the intervention of money.

Of all the traffic in which civilized society is involved, that of human labor is perhaps the most detrimental. From the state of serfdom to the receipt of wages may be a step in human progress; but it is certainly full time for taking a new step out of the hiring system.

Our outward exertions are in the first instance directed to the soil, and as our ultimate aim is to furnish an instance of self-sustaining cultivation without the subjugation of either men or cattle, or the use of foul animal manures, we have at the outset to encounter struggles and oppositions somewhat formidable. Until the land is restored to its pristine fertility by the annual return of its own green crops, as sweet and animating manures, the human hand and simple implement cannot wholly supersede the employment of machinery and cattle. So long as cattle are used in agriculture, it is very evident that man will remain a slave, whether he be proprietor or hireling. The driving of cattle beyond their natural and pleasurable exertion; the waiting upon them as cook and chambermaid three parts of the year; the excessive labor of mowing, curing, and housing hay, and of collecting other fodder, and the large extra quantity of land needful to keep up this system, form a continuation of unfavorable circumstances which must depress the human affections

The Small Dining-Room
Around this table the philosophers discussed their deepest problems

so long as it continues, and overlay them by the injurious and extravagant development of the animal and bestial natures in man. It is calculated that if no animal food were consumed, one-fourth of the land now used would suffice for human sustenance. And the extensive tracts of country now appropriated to grazing, mowing, and other modes of animal provision, could be cultivated by and for intelligent and affectionate human neighbors. The sty and the stable too often secure more of the farmer's regard than he bestows on the garden and the children. No hope is there for humanity while Woman is withdrawn from the tender assiduities which adorn her and her household, to the servitudes of the dairy and the flesh pots. If the beasts were wholly absent from man's neighborhood, the human population might be at least four times as dense as it now is without raising the price of land. This would give to the country all the advantages of concentration without the vices which always spring up in the dense city.

Debauchery of both the earthly soil and the human body is the result of this cattle keeping. The land is scourged for crops to feed the animals, whose ordures are used under the erroneous supposition of restoring lost fertility; disease is thus infused into the human body; stimulants and medicines are resorted to for relief, which end in a precipitation of the original evil to a more disastrous depth. These misfortunes which affect not only the body, but by reaction rise to the sphere of the soul, would be avoided, or at least in part, by the disuse of animal food. Our diet is therefore strictly the pure and bloodless kind. No animal substances, neither flesh, butter, cheese, eggs, nor milk, pollute our table or corrupt our bodies, neither tea, coffee, molasses, nor rice, tempts us beyond the bounds of indigenous productions. Our sole beverage is pure fountain water. The native grains, fruits, herbs, and roots, dressed with the utmost cleanliness and regard to their purpose of edifying a healthful body, furnish the pleasantest refections and in the greatest variety requisite to the supply of the various organs. The field, the orchard, the garden, in their bounteous products of wheat, rye, barley, maize, oats, buckwheat, apples, pears, peaches, plums, cherries, currants, berries, potatoes, peas, beans, beets, carrots, melons, and other vines, yield an ample store for human nutrition, without dependence on foreign climes, or the degeneration of shipping and trade. The almost inexhaustible variety of the several stages and sorts of vegetable growth, and the several modes of preparation, are a full answer to the question which is often put by those who have never ventured into the region of a pure and chaste diet: "If you give up flesh meat, upon what then can you live?"

Our other domestic habits are in harmony with those of diet. We rise with early dawn, begin the day with cold bathing, succeeded by a music lesson, and then a chaste repast. Each one finds occupation until the meridian meal, when usually some interesting and deep-searching conversation gives rest to the body and development to the mind. Occupation, according to the season and the weather, engages us out of doors or within, until the evening meal, — when we again assemble in social communion, prolonged generally until sunset, when we resort to sweet repose for the next day's activity.

In these steps of reform we do not rely as much on scientific reasoning of physiological skill, as on the Spirit's dictates. The pure soul, by the law of its own nature, adopts a pure diet and cleanly customs; nor needs detailed instruction for daily conduct. On a revision of our proceedings it would seem, that if we were in the right course in our particular instance, the greater part of man's duty consists in leaving alone much that he is in the habit of doing. It is a fasting from the present activity, rather than an increased indulgence in it, which, with patient watchfulness tends to newness of life. "Shall I sip tea or coffee?" the inquiry may be. No; abstain from all ardent, as from alcoholic drinks. "Shall I consume pork, beef, or mutton?" Not if you value health or life. "Shall I stimulate with milk?" No. "Shall I warm my bathing water?" Not if cheerfulness is valuable. "Shall I clothe in many garments?" Not if purity is aimed at. "Shall I prolong my dark hours, consuming animal oil and losing bright daylight in the morning?" Not if a clear mind is an object. "Shall I teach my children the dogmas inflicted on myself, under the pretence that I am transmitting truth?" Nay, if you love them intrude not these between them and the Spirit of all Truth. "Shall I subjugate cattle?" "Shall I trade?" "Shall I claim property in any created thing?" "Shall I interest myself in politics?" To how many of these questions could we ask them deeply enough, could they be heard as having relation to our eternal welfare, would the response be "Abstain"? Be not so active to do, as sincere to be. Being in preference to doing, is the great aim and this comes to us rather by a resigned willingness than a wilful activity; — which is indeed a check to all divine growth. Outward abstinence is a sign of inward fulness; and the only source of true progress is inward. We may occupy ourselves actively in human improvements; — but these unless inwardly well-impelled, never attain to, but rather hinder, divine progress in man. During the utterance of this narrative it has undergone a change in its personal expression which might offend the hypercritical; but we feel assured that you will kindly accept it as unartful offering of both your friends in ceaseless aspiration.

Charles Lane,
A. Bronson Alcott.

'Harvard, Mass.,
   August, 1843.

[1] This was a mistake on Mr. Carter's part, as they ate potatoes freely.

IV - The Man with the Beard

No satisfactory record of Fruitlands could be written without giving an account of Joseph Palmer, the man with the beard. He filled an important place in the life of the Community, and is one of those picturesque characters which must always stand out vividly in the history of Fruitlands. He came of fine, sturdy English stock which emigrated to this country in 1730. His grandfather taught school in Newton, Massachusetts, for twenty years. His father fought in the Revolution, and he himself was a soldier in the War of 1812. He was an eccentric character, but steadfast and upright, and immovable when it came to his principles. Wearing a beard became a fixed idea with him, and neither the law of the land nor the admonitions of the church could make him falter in his determination to claim freedom of action in this respect. He suffered ridicule, insolence, and persecution to a degree that was amazing, and which revealed the fact that in spite of a seemingly greater enlightenment on the part of the public, the same tendency, which drove the people to persecute so-called witches, and Shakers, and harmless persons with a little different viewpoint from their own, was still alive, and ready to flame forth as fiercely as ever.

On one occasion, before the Fruitlands days, he went into a church in Fitchburg where the holy Communion was being celebrated. He knelt with the rest only to be given the shock of humiliation at being ignored and passed over by the officiating clergyman. Cut to the quick at such injustice, and with the blood surging to his face, he arose and strode up to the Communion table where the Sacraments were, and lifting the cup to his lips drank from it, and turning to the shocked and abashed clergyman and his congregation shouted in a loud voice and with flashing eyes: "I love my Jesus as well, and better, than any of you do!"

A beard at that time was only worn by the Jews, and that was the real reason for this persecution, and it caused him to be called "Old Jew Palmer," though there was not a drop of Jewish blood in his veins. He carried on his farm at No Town very successfully and sold his beef at the Fitchburg Market. No Town was a "gore" of unreclaimed land outside of Fitchburg and Leominster in old Colonial days, a large tract of which had been granted to Captain Noah Wiswell, his maternal grandfather, by the General Court of the Province of Massachusetts for bravery in the wars against the Indians. Joseph Palmer inherited it. It belonged to no township, and therefore was not taxed. So when he married the widow Tenney rumors circulated through Fitchburg that the marriage was not legal because he did not publish the banns at the meeting-house according to law, there being no meeting-house at No Town. But investigation proved the marriage legal because he had published the banns in his own handwriting on a large piece of paper which he had tacked to the trunk of a fine old pine tree which grew near his house.

Joseph Palmer's wife before her first marriage was Nancy Thompson. She was a third cousin to Count Rumford, who was Benjamin Thompson, of Woburn, in Colonial days, but who returned to England after the evacuation of the British, and on account of services rendered to the Government was knighted by George III, and afterward given the title of Count Rumford by the reigning king of Bavaria, and was well known throughout Europe as a scientist, philosopher, and savant.

A reporter of the *Boston Daily Globe* in 1884 interviewed Joseph Palmer's son. Dr. Palmer, of Fitchburg, and herein are inserted extracts from the interview: —

"The older inhabitants of Harvard, Sterling, Leominster, Fitchburg, and other neighboring towns can remember 'Old Jew Palmer,' who fifty years ago was persecuted, despised, jeered at, regarded almost as a fiend incarnate;

who was known far and wide as a human monster, and with whose name mothers used to frighten their children when they were unruly.

"'Old Jew Palmer,' as he was universally called, was the most abused and persecuted man these parts ever knew, and all because he insisted upon wearing a beard. But many who in those days looked upon the subject of this sketch as a social outcast have lived to see whiskers common and fashionable.

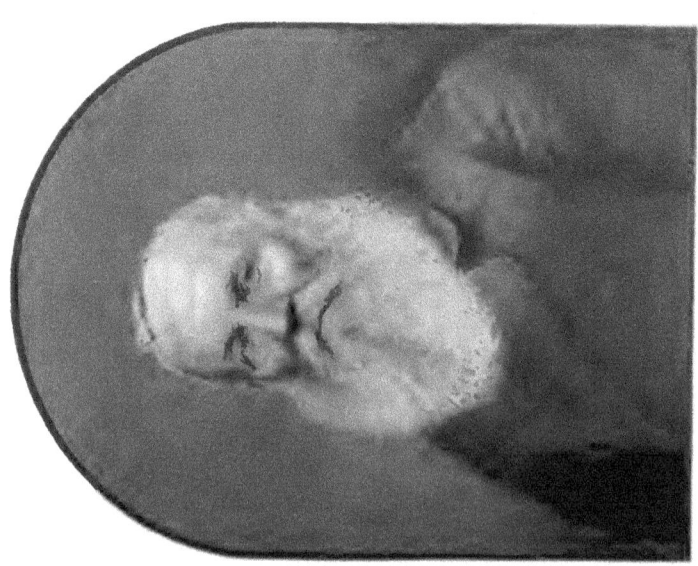

Joseph Palmer and Nancy Palmer

"With a view of getting at the facts of the persecution of Mr. Palmer but fifty years ago, his only son, Dr. Thomas Palmer, a well-known dentist of Fitchburg, was interviewed, and the doctor talked earnestly and vigorously about his father's career, for he had seen the time when his schoolmates shunned him and made his boyhood days miserable, railing at him because his father wore a beard. But now the doctor looks back upon those days proudly, as he realizes that his sire was right and that the world has indorsed the ways and ideas of the old man, instead of the old man bowing to the absurd whim of the world."

Said Dr. Palmer: —

"Father left No Town early in the thirties and moved to Fitchburg into a house where the City Hall now stands. He wore at that time a long beard, and he and Silas Lamson, an old scythe-snath maker of Sterling, were the only men known in this section of the country as wearing beards. Everybody shaved clean in those days, and to wear whiskers in any form was worse than a disgrace, it was a sin. Father was hooted at on the street, talked about at the grocery, intimidated by his fellow-men and labored with by the clergy to shave, but to no purpose. The stronger the opposition, the firmer his determination. He was accosted once by Rev. George Trask, the anti-tobacconist, who said indignantly: 'Palmer, why don't you shave and not go round looking like the devil?' He replied: 'Mr. Trask, are you not mistaken in your comparison of personages? I have never seen a picture of the ruler of the sulphurous regions with much of a beard, but if I remember correctly, Jesus wore a beard not unlike mine.' That squelched Trask and he left.

"Well, public sentiment against the man and beard grew stronger, and personal violence was threatened. One day, as father was coming out of the old Fitchburg Hotel, where he had been to carry some provision, he then being in the butchering business, he was seized by four men, whose names I have not in mind now, who were armed with shears, lather, and razor, their intention being to shave him, as the sentiment of the populace was that that beard must come off at the hands of the wearer, possibly at the hands of some one, anyway. Why, there are men living to-day, old associates of his, who still cling to that old idea and will not wear a beard. These four men laid violent hands upon him and threw him heavily on the stone steps, badly hurting his back. The assaulted party was very muscular, and struggled to free himself, but to no purpose, until he drew from his vest pocket an old, loose-jointed jack-knife, with which he struck out left and right and stabbed two of them in the legs, when the assailants precipitately departed without cutting a hair. He was afterwards arrested for committing an unprovoked assault, and ordered by Justice Brigham to pay a fine, which he refused to do, as he claimed to be acting for the maintenance of a principle. He was thrown into jail, where he remained over a year. He was lodged with the debtors. One day Jailer Bellows came in with several men to shave him. He threw himself on his back in his bunk, and when they approached, he struck out with his feet, and after he had kicked over a few of them they let him and his beard alone. He wrote letters to the Worcester *Spy*, complaining of the treatment the prisoners received, which I used to carry to the office for him, receiving them when I carried him his meals, for we hired a tenement next to the jail. For this the jailer put him in a sort of dungeon down below, and one day when I went to the jail, he heard my step and called out: 'Thomas, tie a stone to a string and swing it by the window so that I can catch it'; which I did, and pulled up a letter for High Sheriff Williams, in which he complained of his treatment. The sheriff ordered him back to his old quarters. Why, old Dr. Williams of Leominster told father once that he ought to be prosecuted and imprisoned for wearing a beard. In after years, when whiskers became fashionable, father met a minister who had upbraided him years before for wearing them, and as this same minister had rather a luxuriant growth, he went up to the man of God and stroking his whiskers, said to him, 'Knoweth that thy redeemer liveth?' He claimed to be the redeemer of the beard.

"Father was a reformer; was early in the field as an anti-slavery man and as a total abstinence advocate. He was well acquainted with Phillips, Garrison, and other prominent Abolitionists. I remember going with him once to an anti-slavery convention in Boston. As we walked up Washington Street, the people would stop, then run ahead, wait for us to come up, and finally the crowd around us was so great that the police had to come to the rescue. Why was it? Oh, it was the same old beard. It was so unusual to see a man wearing one, and especially such a one as he sported. Why, he was looked upon as a monstrosity. When asked once why he wore it, he said he would tell if any one could tell him why some men would, from fifty-two to three hundred and sixty-five times a year, scrape their face from their nose to their neck. He never would furnish liquor for men in the hay-field, and for this reason had hard work to gather crops; but they would have rotted before he would have backed down and sacrificed his principle. He was the first man in this section to give up that old custom. He was interested in all reformatory ideas, and was associated with A. Bronson Alcott in forming that Community in Harvard at Fruitlands which had for its object a more quiet and unostentatious way of living than the world offered. He went to Harvard in 1843. The Community did not flourish, and father bought the farm. Ralph Waldo Emerson, as trustee, at that time held the deed of 'Fruitlands.' I remember that when father refused to furnish liquor for the hay-makers he had to hire boys. One mother refused to let her lad work for him, saying that 'He was too mean to allow the boys a little liquor'!

"Such was the interesting account given by the venerable doctor of a condition of affairs existing in this community but a comparatively few years ago; but the average person of to-day would not believe, without a full explanation of the sentiment prevailing at that time, that within so recent a period a man would not only be insulted and persecuted, but actually mobbed, as was the victim of this foolish and intolerant community."

While in prison Palmer kept a diary, in which, under date of July 21, 1830, occurs this account of the sort of persecution he had from the two fellow-prisoners who occupied the same cell with him. One of them asserted that if the other prisoner would attack him and cut his beard off, he would look on all the time and then swear that it had never happened, and that anyway he could get enough money collected anywhere on the street to pay the damages for the act. The jailer coming to the door at this moment overheard the remark and with a resounding oath agreed with him, and added, "And pretty quick, too!" Then he began to curse and swear at Palmer, and vowed that they would get his beard off soon, and even suggested that the other prisoners should cut it off of him in his sleep. One of these prisoners was named Dike. The jailer continued to pour volley after volley of oaths at the unfortunate man, and finally spat on him repeatedly. This happened when Palmer's cell was being whitewashed and the three inmates were temporarily removed to another cell. When they were taken back to their customary quarters, Dike found that the jailer had taken his razor away, which turned his wrath in a new direction, and Palmer writes that as a result "Before bedtime, he was as good as a man ought to be to another, and talked very freely with me on the Power and Goodness of God and on the Holy Scriptures."

Here is an entry on Wednesday, September 22, 1830: —

"I called out to some one in the hall. Wildes, the jailer, opened the door in the entry next to my door and said: 'What do you want?' I was just going to ask him for a little water to use until I could get some tea from Wilson, and he let a pail full come in at the door, with great force. It didn't wet me much, as I see it was coming, and having seen them throw cider and water in the prisoners' faces before. It caused me to start so quickly that there did but little go into my face, and on my clothes, but it went more than half the length of the room. I split three crackers and put them to soak where there was considerable water standing on the floor, as I could see no chance of getting any more soon. I got a quart jug filled with water out of the other room to wet some bread which was all the water or drink of any kind that I had since last Thursday morning when I used the last of my tea, and I had tried ever since last Sunday morning to get some and could not. I thought I must suffer very much soon if there wasn't some attention, and being satisfied that there were some in Prison who were suffering greatly, I thought it time to give a signal of distress to the Public, which I immediately did by the cry of murder in the Gaol, which I continued at the window that somebody might come up while the door was open that would grant some assistance for the pay. About seven o'clock just as I was going to take my crackers off the floor. Bellows and Wildes came into the room and several others. I stepped to the table and took the lines I had written to send to Mr. Wilson, and asked them if I could get any one of them to go for me if I would pay them for it. Bellows said, 'Yes, I'll take care of you!' Bellows and Wildes then seized me by the collar, shook and jarred me with great fury through the entries, and dragged me down the stairs. I tried to speak to the people who stood by to take the paper I had in my hand to carry to Mr. Wilson. Bellows then took me by the hair and shook me furiously as I suppose to prevent my speaking to them. I then cried Murder. He then let me go, and I told them that I wanted to get some person to take the paper I had in my hand and go about 100 rods of an errand, and I would pay them well for it, for I hadn't had anything to drink since last week, nor I couldn't get any. They put me into the South Middle room below and gave me a pail of water. I told Wildes and C. B. that I wanted they should let me have my things, for I hadn't eaten anything since yesterday morning. They took the other three prisoners out of the room and shut the blinds."

Palmer was kept in solitary confinement from September 22 to December 25.

December 30, 1830.

"In the afternoon Calvin Willard, Ashel Bellows, Wildes, and Lawyer Goodwin, with four or five other gentlemen, came in. Willard said, 'How do you do, Palmer?' I said, pretty tolerable well for me except I have got a bad cold. One of the men, which I took to be Esqre. Weed said to me: 'Why don't you go out? What do you stay here for? Why don't you pay up the demand and go out?' I said I have no way to pay it. Goodwin said: 'A man from Fitchburg told me today that he has from ten to fifteen hundred dollars property.' Willard said: 'I always took him to be a man of property.' One of the men said: 'I think there ought to be some measures taken to secure the board if he stops here.' I said: I board myself and have hard work to get it in here for the money. One said: 'How much was your fine?' I said, Ten dollars, I believe it was."

Saturday, January 1, 1831.

"Since the first of December I haven't bought me anything from Bellows, and they haven't brought me anything but eight Bushels and one hod of coal, and they used two Bushels of that when they whitewashed the room, except what I took to make one fire. Thomas brought me my water. I was out of my room three and a half days to have it whitewashed, and I have now a half Bushel of coal which brings it to seven and a half Bushels I have burnt the past month while I was in the room."

April 11, 1831.

"Food for the day: —
"Breakfast: 5 ounces of brown bread
"Dinner: 5¼ ounces of brown bread, 3½ ounces of beef meat, 3½ ounces of potato, 3¾ ounces of soup."

"He far out-stayed his sentence because he had to pay for all his food, drink, and coal for heating, and he considered they cheated him, so he refused to go. The sheriff and jailers, tired of having him there, begged him to leave. Even his mother, Margaret Palmer, wrote to him 'Not to be so set.' But nothing could move him. He said they had put him in there, and they would have to take him out, as he would not walk out. They finally carried him out in his chair and placed it on the sidewalk."

Shortly after leaving the jail at Worcester Palmer heard of the proposed Community of Fruitlands, and being much interested in all reforms, he offered to run the farm without pay and went there at the very start. He took some fine old furniture with him from No Town to help furnish the house, and whenever anything was needed in the way of farm implements, etc., he would drive over to No Town and bring it back with him. When the Community of Fruitlands failed, he bought the place and carried on a strange sort of Community of his own for upwards of twenty years. Emerson visited him afterwards, and a motley collection of reformers, wayfarers, and a host of tramps found a welcome by his fireside.

Any one driving by the old North Leominster graveyard will see a stone monument adorned with the head of a man with a flowing beard. On it is written: —

JOSEPH PALMER
died
October 30, 1875
Aged 84 years, 5 months

Underneath the carved head is written: —

Persecuted for
Wearing the Beard

V - Summer Sunshine

It was now July and all the days were full of healthful occupations — the weather was perfect. The philosophers had planted three mulberry trees next the front door, and they had set out apple trees and pear trees below the house on the slope of the hill. They put the mulberry trees so near the house that when they grew, the roots almost unsettled the foundations, and the fruit trees were planted in just the wrong place to permit of luxuriant growth; but they never knew it, and at the time they pictured to themselves the full-grown trees with branches overladen with the luscious ripening fruit. And now they all had gotten their linen suits designed by Mr. Lane: — loose trousers, tunic-ed coats and broad-brimmed linen hats like Southern planters. The Alcott girls, Anna, Beth, Louisa, and three-year-old baby May were in linen bloomers, and so were Mrs. Alcott (protesting!) and poor Miss Page, who was summarily dismissed from Fruitlands for having eaten fish.

Many visitors came and went. Parker Pillsbury often came, his mind full of the anti-slavery question. The Concord circle of friends looked in upon them off and on, and Channing spoke afterwards of conversations held in a small dining-room next to the front door, and, as Mr. Sanborn says in his account of it, "The library of rare books from London stood proudly on its hundred feet of new shelves in the small front entry of the old house, proclaiming the atmosphere of 'Mind and Letters.'"

The Refectory also used as a Kitchen

Emerson came and afterwards wrote in his "Journal" on July 8, 1843: —

"The sun and the evening sky do not look calmer than Alcott and his family at Fruitlands. They seemed to have arrived at the fact — to have got rid of the show, and so to be serene. Their manners and behavior in the house and the field were those of superior men — of men at rest. What had they to conceal? What had they to exhibit? And it seemed so high an attainment that I thought — as often before, so now more, because they had a fit home, or the picture was fitly framed — that these men ought to be maintained in their place by the country for its culture.

"Young men and young maidens, old men and women, should visit them and be inspired. I think there is as much merit in beautiful manners as in hard work. I will not prejudge them successful. They look well in July; we will see them in December. I know they are better for themselves than as partners. One can easily see that they have yet to settle several things. Their saying that things are clear, and they sane, does not make them so. If they will in very deed be lovers, and not selfish; if they will serve the town of Harvard, and make their neighbors feel them as benefactors wherever they touch them, — they are as safe as the sun."

Mr. Sanborn, referring to the remark, "We will see them in December," says: "This passage indicates that Emerson with his fatal gift of perception had long since seen the incongruity between Alcott and Lane. At this time all was still fair weather at the Fruitlands Eden, although the burden of too much labor, of which Lane had written to Thoreau in June, had been falling more and more heavily on Mrs. Alcott and her daughters, Anna, then twelve, and Louisa, not quite eleven. As they did so much of the domestic drudgery, Mrs. Alcott doubtless thought it no more than right that her English guests, both there and at Concord, during the seven months that Lane and his son were in their household, should pay their share of the family expenses."

The house at times was very overcrowded and the children had their beds up in the garret. But Anna begged hard for a tiny room adjoining Mrs. Alcott's, and great was the joy she took in it. Of course it all was very primitive. The men bathed in the brook in the early morning and the shower-baths that Anna speaks of in her diary were accomplished thus: — rough clothes-horses covered with sheets were put in a circle and the bathers stood hidden within, while Mr. Alcott, mounted on some wooden steps, poured water from a pitcher through a sieve on their head. (This was told the author by an old lady who when very young went to visit the children.)

Hired laborers and beasts of burden were against the principles of the Community, but in order to make headway against the advancing season they seemed to be a necessity. This concession, however, troubled the philosophers, and it was decided to carry out the original plan and rely wholly on the spade instead of the plough, even at a cost of valuable time. The results were rather disastrous: Charles Lane's hands became sore and painful, and lame backs seriously interfered with progress. Sobered by this new experience, the philosophers met in conclave, and as a result Joseph Palmer, who always came to the rescue in trying situations, went to No Town and brought back his plough and yoke of oxen, as he called it — it really was an ox and a cow which he had trained to work together. Besides the outdoor work much writing was done indoors. Charles Lane and Bower wrote prolifically to different papers. *The Herald of Freedom,* the *Vermont Telegraph* and the *New York Tribune* of that summer are full of their writings.

Mr. Alcott's Diary furnishes clear evidence of his purposes and hopes: —

"I would abstain from the fruits of oppression and blood, and am seeking means of entire independence. This, were I not holden by penury unjustly, would be possible. One miracle we have wrought nevertheless, and shall soon work all of them: Our wine is water, flesh, bread — drugs, fruits; and we defy meekly the satyrs all, and Aesculapians. The Soul's banquet is an art divine....This Beast named Man has yet most costly tastes, and must first be transformed into a very Man, regenerate in appetite and desire, before the earth shall be restored to fruitfulness, and redeemed from the curse of his cupidity. Then shall the toils of the farm become eloquent and invigorating leisures; Man shall grow his orchards and plant his gardens — an husbandman truly, sowing and reaping in hope, and a partaker in his hope. Labor will be attractive; life will not be worn in anxious and indurating toils; it will be a scene of mixed leisure, recreation, labor, culture. The soil, grateful then for man's generous usage, debauched no more by foul ordures, nor worn by cupidities, shall recover its primeval virginity, bearing on its bosom the standing bounties which a sober and liberal Providence ministers to his heed — sweet and invigorating growths, for the health and comfort of the grower."

Mr. Sanborn, commenting on this, remarks: —

"It was in the spirit of the passages just quoted from Alcott's diary...and not from the ordinary Fourieristic notions about attractions and destinies and cooperative housekeeping that Alcott undertook his experiment at 'Fruitlands.'"

Alcott's theory of human life was thus set down in his Diary: —

"I have been (as is ever the habit of my mind) striving to apprehend the real in the seeming, to strip ideas of their adventitious phrases, and behold them in their order and powers. I have sought to penetrate the showy terrestrial to find the heavenly things; I have tried to translate into ideas the language and images of spirit, and thus to read God in his works. The outward I have seen as the visible type of the inward. Ever doth this same nature double its divine form, and stand forth — now before the inner, now before the outer sense of man — at once substance and form, image and idea, so that God shall never slip wholly from consciousness of the Soul. Faith apprehends his agency, even in the meanest and most seemingly trivial act, whenever organ or matter undergo change of function or mode of form, — Spirit being all in all. Amidst all tumults and discomfitures, all errors and evils, Faith discerns the subtle bond that marries opposite natures, clinging to that which holds all in harmonious union. It unites opposites; it demolishes opposing forces. It melts all solid and obstinate matters. It makes fluid the material universe. It hopes even in despair, believes in the midst of doubts, apprehends stability and order even in confusion and anarchy, and, while all without is perturbed and wasting, it possesses itself in quietude and repose within. It abides in the unswerving, is mighty in the omnipotent, and enduring in the eternal. The soul quickened by its agency, though borne on the waves of the mutable and beset by the winds of error and the storms of evil, shall ride securely under this directing hand to the real and the true. In the midst of change, it shall remain unchanged. For to such a faith is the divine order of God made known. All visible things are but manifestations of this order. Nature, with all its change, is but the activity of this power. It flows around and obeys the invisible self-anchored spirit. Mutability to such a vision, is as the eddy that spirit maketh around its own self-circling agency, revealing alike in the smallest ripple and the mightiest surges the power that stirreth at the centre."

VI - Father Hecker's Description of Fruitlands

[Isaac Thomas Hecker was born in New York in 1819. Two years after his experience at Brook Farm and Fruitlands he entered the Roman Catholic church, and in 1849 he was ordained a priest. Later he founded the Paulist Fathers. He died in 1888. The following extracts are taken from a contemporary record of his impressions while in the socialistic community.]

"Fruitlands," so called because fruit was to be the principal staple of daily food, and to be cultivated on the farm, was a spot well chosen; it was retired, breathing quiet and tranquillity. No neighboring dwelling obstructed the view of Nature, and it lay some distance even from a bypath road, in a delightful solitude. The house, somewhat dilapidated, was on the slope of a slowly ascending hill; stretched before it was a small valley under cultivation, with fields of corn, potatoes, and meadow. In the distance loomed up on high "Cheshire's haughty hill," Monadnoc. Such was the spot chosen by men inspired to live a holier life, to bring Eden once more upon earth. These men were impressed with the religiousness of their enterprise. When the first load of hay was driven into the barn and the first fork was about to be plunged into it, one of the family took off his hat and said, "I take off my hat, not that I reverence the bam more than other places, but because this is the first fruit of our labor." Then a few moments were given to silence, that holy thought might be awakened.

July 7, 1843. Brook Farm.

I go to Mr. Alcott's next Tuesday, if nothing happens. I have had three pairs of coarse pants and a coat made for me. It is my intention to commence work as soon as I get there. I will gradually simplify my dress without making any sudden difference, although it would be easier to make a radical and thorough change at once than piece by piece. But this will be a lesson in patient perseverance to me. All our difficulties should be looked at in such a light as to improve and elevate our minds,

I can hardly prevent myself from saying how much I shall miss the company of those I love and associate with here. But I must go. I am called with a stronger voice. This is a different trial from any I have ever had. I have never had that of leaving kindred, but now I have that of leaving those whom I love from affinity. If I wished to live a life the most gratifying to me, and in agreeable company, I certainly would remain here. Here are refining amusements, cultivated persons — and one whom I have not spoken of, one who is too much to me to speak of, one who would leave all for me. Alas! him I must leave to go.

Isaac T. Hecker

"[In this final sentence, as it now stands in the diary and as we have transcribed it, occurs one of those efforts of which we have spoken to obliterate the traces of this early attachment. 'Him' was originally written 'her,' but the *r* has been lengthened to an *m*, and the *e* dotted, both with care which overshot their mark, by an almost imperceptible hair's breadth. If the nature of this attachment were not so evident from other sources, we should have left such passages unquoted; fearing lest they might be misunderstood. As it is, the light they cast seems to us to throw up into fuller proportions the kind and extent of the renunciations to which Isaac Hecker was called before he had arrived at any clear view of the end to which they tended.]" [1]

Fruitlands, July 12.

Last evening I arrived here. After tea I went out in the fields and raked hay for an hour in company with the persons here. We returned and had a conversation on clothing. Some very fine things were said by Mr. Alcott and Mr. Lane. In most of their thoughts I coincide; they are the same which of late have much occupied my mind. Alcott said that "to Emerson the world was a lecture room, to Brownson a rostrum."

This morning after breakfast a conversation was held on Friendship and its laws and conditions. Mr. Alcott places Innocence first; Lamed, Thoughtfulness; I, Seriousness; Lane, Fidelity.

July 13.

This morning after breakfast there was held a conversation on the Highest Aim. Mr. Alcott said it was Integrity; I, Harmonic being; Lane, Progressive being; Larned, Annihilation of self; Bower, Repulsion of the evil in us. Then there was a confession of the obstacles which prevent us from attaining the highest aim. Mine was the doubt whether the light is light; not want of will to follow, or light to see.

July 17.

I cannot understand what it is that leads me, or what I am after. Being is incomprehensible. What shall I be led to? Is there a being whom I may marry and who would be the means of opening my eyes? Sometimes I think so, but it appears impossible. Why should others tell me that it is so, and will be so, in an unconscious way, as Lamed did on Sunday last, and as others have done before him? Will I be led home? It strikes me these people here, Alcott and Lane, will be a great deal to me. I do not know but they may be what I am looking for, or the answer to that in me which is asking.

Can I say it? I believe it should be said. Here I cannot end. They are too near me; they do not awaken in me that sense of their high superiority which would keep me here to be bettered, to be elevated. They have much, very much. I desire Mr. Alcott's strength of self-denial, and the unselfishness of Mr. Lane in money matters. In both these they are far my superior. I would be meek, humble, and sit at their feet that I might be as they are. They do not understand me, but if I am what my consciousness, my heart, lead me to feel, — if I am not deceived, — why, then I can wait. Yes, patiently wait. Is not this the first time since I have been here that I have recovered myself? Do I not feel that I have something to receive here, to add to, to increase my highest life, which I have never felt anywhere else?

Is this sufficient to keep me here? If I can prophesy, I must say no. I feel that it will not fill my capacity. Oh God! strengthen my resolution. Let me not waver, and continue my life. But I am sinful. Oh forgive my sins! what shall I do, O Lord! that they may be blotted out? Lord could I only blot them out from my memory, nothing would be too great or too much.

July 18.

I have thought of my family this afternoon, and the happiness and love with which I might return to them. To leave them, to give up the idea of living with them again. — Can I entertain that idea? Still, I cannot conceive how I can engage in business, share the practices, and indulge myself with the food and garmenture of our home and city. To return home, were it possible for me, would most probably not only stop my progress, but put me back. It is useless for me to speculate upon my future. Put dependence on the spirit which leads me, be faithful to it, work and leave results to God. If the question should be asked me, whether I would give up my kindred and business and follow out this spirit life, or return and enjoy them both, I could not hesitate a moment, for they would not compare — there would be no room for choice. What I do I must do, for it is not I that do it; it is the spirit. What that spirit may be is a question I cannot answer. What it leads me to do will be the only evidence of its character. I feel as impersonal as a stranger to it. I ask who are you? Where are you going to take me? Why me? Why not some one else? Alas! I cry, who am I and what does this mean? And I am lost in wonder.

Saturday, July 21.

Yesterday, after supper, a conversation took place between Mr. Alcott, Mr. Lane, and myself; the subject was my position with regard to my family, my duty, and my position here. Mr. Alcott asked for my first impressions as regards the hinderances that I have noted since coming here. I told him candidly they were:

First, his want of frankness; 2d, his disposition to separateness rather than win co-operation with the aims in his own mind; 3d, his family who prevent his immediate plans of reformation; 4th, the fact that his place has very little fruit on it, when it was and is their desire that fruit should be the principal part of their diet; 5th, my fear that they have too decided tendency toward literature and writing for the prosperity and success of their, enterprise.

[From this on, the diary is full of questionings and unrest. Should he return to his family and live as an ordinary man, or should he listen to the urge of the spirit within and seek further for the light? These and other questions pursued him night and day. Finally he came to a conclusion.]

July 23.

I will go home, be true to the spirit with the help of God, and wait for further light and strength...I feel that I cannot live at this place as I would. This is not the place for my soul...My life is not theirs. They have been the means of giving me much light on myself, but I feel I would live and progress more in a different atmosphere.

[It is interesting to note that after his return home he continued the diet which was used at Fruitlands. The account of his life states: "One of the first noteworthy things revealed by the diary, which from this time on was kept with less regularity than before, — is that Isaac not only maintained his abstemious habits after his return, but increased their vigor."]

August 30.

If the past nine months or more are any evidence, I find that I can live on very simple diet — grains, fruit, and nuts. I have just commenced to eat the latter; I drink pure water. So far I have had wheat ground and made into unleavened bread, but as soon as we get in a new lot, I shall try it in the grain.

Hecker had evidently at this time a practical conviction of the truth of a principle which, in after years, he repeated in the form of a maxim of the Transcendentalists: "A gross feeder will never be a central thinker." It is a truth of the spiritual no less than of the intellectual order. A little later we come upon the following profession of a vegetarian faith: —

"Reasons for not eating animal food.

"It does not feed the spirit.

"It stimulates the propensities.

"It is taking animal life when the other kingdoms offer sufficient and better increment. Slaughter strengthens the lower instincts. It is the chief cause of the slavery of the kitchen.

"It generates in the body the diseases animals are subject to, and encourages in man their bestiality.

"Its odor is offensive and its appearance unaesthetic."

Mr. Alcott's death in 1888 was the occasion of reminiscences from Father Hecker, from which a few extracts are taken: —

"When did I first know him? Hard to remember. He was the head of Fruitlands, as Ripley was of Brook Farm. They were entirely different men. Diogenes and his tub would have been Alcott's ideal if he had carried it out. Ripley's ideal would have been Epictetus. Ripley would have taken with him the good things of this life. Alcott would have rejected them all."

"How did he receive you at Fruitlands?"

"Very kindly, but from mixed and selfish motives. I suspect he wanted me because he thought I would bring money to the Community. Lane was entirely unselfish."

"Alcott was a man of great intellectual gifts or acquirements. His knowledge came chiefly from experience and instinct. He had an insinuating and persuasive way with him."

"What if he had been a Catholic, and thoroughly sanctified?"

"He could have been nothing but a hermit like those of the fourth century — he was naturally and constitutionally so odd. Emerson, Alcott, and Thoreau were three consecrated cranks."

Here also are two interesting passages from the "Life of Father Hecker," and a few memoranda of private conversations: —

"Somebody once described 'Fruitlands' as a place where Mr. Alcott looked benign and talked philosophy, while Mrs. Alcott and the children did the work. Still to look benign is a good deal for a man to do persistently in an adverse world, indifferent for the most part to the charms of 'divine philosophy,' and Mr. Alcott persevered in that exercise until his latest day."

"He was unquestionably one of those who like to sit upon a platform," wrote at the time of his death, one who knew Alcott well, "and he may have liked to feel that his venerable aspect had the effect of a benediction." "But with this mild criticism, censure of him is well-nigh exhausted."

"Fruitlands was very different from Brook Farm — far more ascetic."

"You didn't like it?"

"Yes; but they did not begin to satisfy me. I said to them: If you had the Eternal here, all right, I would be with you."

"Had they no notion of hereafter?"

"No, nothing definite. Their idea was human perfection. They set out to demonstrate what man can do in the way of the supremacy of the spiritual over the animal; All right, I said, I agree with you fully. I admire your asceticism; it is nothing new to me; I have practiced it a long time myself. If you can get the Everlasting out of my mind, I 'm yours. But I know that I am going to live forever."

"What did Mr. Alcott say when you left?"

"He went to Lane and said, 'Well, Hecker has flunked out. He hadn't the courage to persevere. He's a coward.' But Lane said, 'No; you're mistaken. Hecker is right. He wanted more than we had to give him.'"

[1] Walter Elliott's Life of Father Hecker.

VII - Anna Alcott's Diary at Fruitlands, 1843

This morning I rose pretty early. After breakfast I read and wrote stories. In the afternoon I wrote some letters, And the following ode to Louisa: —

>Louisa dear
>   With love sincere
>Accept this little gift from me.
>   It is with pleasure
>   I send this treasure
>And with it send much love to thee.
>
>   Sister dear
>   Never fear.
>God will help you if you try.
>   Do not despair,
>   But always care
>To be good and love to try.

June 6, 1843.

Having been busy helping arrange things for moving last Thursday, we left Concordia later for Harvard. I walked part of the way, the distance being 14 miles from Concord to Harvard. I felt sad at the thought of leaving Concord and all my little friends, the birth-place of Abba where I had spent many happy hours; but Father and Mother and my dear sisters were going with me, and that would make me happy anywhere, I think. We arrived at our new home late in the afternoon. Our first load of furniture had come before us. We found Christy, Wood Abraham, and William all here. Mother was well pleased with the house. There is no beauty in the house itself, but to look out on three sides, you can see mountains, hills, woods, and in some places the Still River may be seen through the trees. At some distance are the Shaker Villages. On the whole, I like the house very well. After eating our supper we fixed our beds and went early to bed. Having no time to put up the bedsteads, we slept on the floor which made my back lame. Friday and Saturday in working and arranging the house in order. To-day in the morning I cleared the table and washed the dishes, being washing day. I washed with Mother and got dinner. In the afternoon I sewed and read. I did not do much this evening, for I went to bed when I had finished the dishes. The men have been planting to-day com, and cutting wood and fixing round about the house out of doors.

Wednesday, 11.

I began my school to-day. We commenced by singing, "When the day with rosy light." It seemed so pleasant to sing with my sisters. After singing I wrote my journal and the girls wrote in their books. They then studied arithmetic lesson. I then gave them a recess, after which they spelt, read and Louisa recited geography. At eleven the school was dismissed. In the afternoon I sewed for my dolly and took care of Abba, then all went to walk in the woods. It was quiet and beautiful there and I felt a calmness in myself. The sun was shining and the birds were singing in the branches of the high trees. It was so beautiful it seemed as if God was near me. I made some oak leaf wreaths, one for father and one for mother, and stuck flowers in them. They looked very pretty indeed. Then we returned from our walk and prepared for supper. In the evening I sang with Christy, William, mother, and sisters.

Thursday, 8.

To-day I gave the children lessons this morning. In the afternoon I wrote. Christy is going to teach me arithmetic and composition, and the subject upon which I am to write is our plan of life. The part I wrote on to-day was flesh-eating. I will write it in here.

COMPOSITION

Life was given to the animals not to be destroyed by men, but to make them happy, and that they might enjoy life. But men are not satisfied with slaying the innocent creatures, but they eat them and so make their bodies of flesh meat. O how many happy lives have been destroyed and how many lov-

ABBA MAY ALCOTT

LOUISA MAY ALCOTT

ANNA BRONSON ALCOTT

ing families have been separated to please an unclean appetite of men! Why were the fruits, berries and vegetables given us if it was intended that we should eat flesh? I am sure it was not. We enjoy the beautiful sights and thoughts God has given us in peace. Why not let them do the same? We have souls to feel and think with, and as they have not the same power of thinking, they should be allowed to live in peace and not made to labour so hard and be beaten so much. Then to eat them! eat what has had life and feeling to make the body of the innocent animals! If treated kindly, they would be kind and tame and love men, but as they now are abused and cruelly treated they do not feel the feeling of "love" towards men. Besides flesh is not clean food, and when there is beautiful juicy fruits who can be a flesh-eater?

In the evening I sang again as I did last night.

Friday, 9.

After breakfast, it being my day for dishes, I cleared up the table. At eleven I had my composition lesson. In the afternoon I sewed, read and played. I sewed in the evening and went to bed early.

Saturday, 10.

This morning father and Mr. Lane went to visit the Shakers in Harvard town. I did the chamber work and then worked and made some bread for dinner, and prepared things ready for it. In the afternoon I laid down, it being very warm out, and read in "Devereux" which pleased me very well. It rained hard and steadily for some time. Father and Mr. Lane returned late in the afternoon. They brought home sweet things they had purchased of the Shakers. We played out on the grounds a little while and then I read and went to bed early.

Sunday, 11.

I read until lo o'clock when we had reading. In the afternoon I read, wrote and had my lessons with Christy. In the evening I received a note from mother accompanied by a roll containing some wafers and some note paper. It was as follows: —

Dear Anna:

I send you a little note paper and a few wafers. You have so much to do lately that I cannot expect you to write often to me, but you must not forget that this is a little duty of yours that gives me a great deal of happiness. This last word reminds me of one of father's beautiful selections to-day.

> "Happiness is like the bird
> That broods above its nest
> And feels beneath its folded wings
> Life's dearest and its best."

I am sure I feel as if I could fold my arms around you all, and say from my heart, "Here is my world within my embrace." Let us try, dear Anna, to make it a good and beautiful world, — that when we are called to leave it we may be fit to join the good and beautiful of another sphere.

> All things proclaim
> In the valley and plain
> That God is near,
> Hills, vales and brooks,
> Sweet words and looks,
> Cast out all fear.
>
> Be the dove of our ark.
> Dear Anna remark

> You're my eldest and best.
> Now you know all the rest,
>
> So farewell dear,
> God is near,
> No evil fear.
> Be happy here.

Mother.

I love to receive letters from mother. She always writes me such dear kind notes.

Monday, 12.

This morning mother baked. I read. Mrs. Lovejoy and Mrs. Willard came here to see mother. In the afternoon I read and wrote, and took a walk with the girls into the woods. In the evening I played and had a shower bath, and then went to bed.

Tuesday, 13.

Mrs. Willard came here and helped mother wash to-day. I helped her some. In the morning I took care of Abba and wrote some. In the afternoon I played, studied, and worked. When Mrs. Willard went home Louisa and I walked with her to learn the way to the house where she lives, for as she took some sewing to do for mother, we wanted to know the way there. We saw some young women braiding straw hats. One of them did it very fast indeed. I think I should like to know how to make hats. Their mother asked us to come and see them (her name is Willard) and mother said we might go. We rode home with Mr. Wyman. When we got here we found two young ladies and a girl who came to see us. They soon went home. I ate my supper and soon after it went to my bed.

Wednesday, 14.

I ironed to-day with mother, and read some. I have not very much to say and so I will write a French fable. [Here a fable is written out in very good French.]

Thursday, 15.

This morning I felt quite unwell, so I laid down and saw Louisa keep school for Lizzie and Abba. I read in "Tales of a Traveller" most all the morning. In the afternoon I had a composition lesson, and then saw father and Abraham - winnow some com and some barley. I then rode to the mill with him and took Abba with us. I never saw a mill working before that I recollect. I sewed when I came home and in the evening talked.

Friday, 16.

Uncle Christy went to Boston this morning. As I was running to bid him good-bye my foot slipped and I fell down on my back. It hurt me a good deal and I had a pain in my side. In the afternoon I went to bed and read. When I got up I fainted. I went to my bed early.

Saturday, 24.

This was Lizzie's birthday. I arose before five o'clock and went with mother, William, and Louisa to the woods where we fixed a little pine tree in the ground and hung up all the presents on it. I then made a wreath for all of us of oak leaves. After breakfast we all, except Abraham, marched to the wood. Mr. Lane took his fiddle with him and we sang first. Then father read a parable, and then this ode which he wrote himself. I will write it on the next page.

Father then asked me what flower I should give Lizzie on her birthday. I said a rose, the emblem of Love and Purity. Father also chose a rose. Louisa said a Lily-of-the-Valley, or innocence, — Mother said she should give her a Forget-me-not, or remembrance. Christy said the trailing Arbutus, the emblem of perseverance. Mr. Lane gave her a piece of moss, or humility. Abba gave her a Wakerobin. I do not know what that means. We then sang. Lizzie looked at her presents and seemed much pleased. Mother gave her a silk thread balloon, I a fan, Louisa a pin-cushion, William a book, Abba a little pitcher. Mr. Lane wrote some lines of poetry which I will write in here: —

TO ELIZABETH

Of all the year the sunniest day
Appointed for thy birth
Is emblem of the longest stay
With us upon the earth.

Now dressed in flowers
The merry hours
Fill up the day and night.
May your whole life

Exempt from strife
Shine forth as calm and bright.
      Fruitlands.

Here is father's: —

BIRTHDAY ODE

I

Here in the grove
With those we love,
In the cool shade
Near mede and glade
With clover tints ore'laid —
A haunt which God ourselves have made —
The trees among
With leaves are hung.
On sylvan plat,
On forest mat,
Near meadow sweet
We take our seat.
While all around
Swells forth the sound
Our happy hearts repeat.

The wood and dell
Our joy to tell
The morning, and
Our peace to share.
Flows by his cool
A balmy school.
The Sun his fires
His kindled iris
Not yet inspires
In midnoon blaze
His scorching rays,
But all is calm and fresh and clear
And all breathes peace around us here.

II

Wake, wake harmonious swell
Along this deep sequestered dell.
Along the grass and brake.
And where the cattle slake
Their thirst, when glides
Adown the sloping sides
In ceaseless frit
The wizard rivulet,
And let the spring maze
Join with violin note
In hymning forth our praise
From forth melodious throat
Our holy joy to tell.

III

Father's here
And Mother dear
And sisters all,
The short and tall,
And Father's friends

Whom Briton lends
To noblest human ends,
With younger arm
From Brooklet farm,
But absent now
At yonder plough
With shining, cleaving share
Upturning to the upper air
The obstinate soil,
The sober son of hardy toil.

IV

Here, here we all repair
Our hope and love to share.
To celebrate
In rustic state
Midst this refulgent whole
The joyful advent of an angel soul
That twice four years ago
Our mundane world to know
Descended from the upper skies
A presence to our veriest eyes
And now before us stands
And asketh at our bounteous hands
Some token of our zeal.
In her most holy weal
Before us stands arrayed
In garments of a maid.
Untainted and pure her soul
As when she left the whole

That doeth this marvelling scene
And. day by day doth preach
The gospel meant for each
That on this solid sphere
For mortal's ear.

V

Then take our tokens all
From great and small
And close that noblest treasure beat
That in your heart doth sleep.
Mind what the spirit saith
And plight therein thy faith,
My very dear Elizabeth,
Nor let the enemy wrest
The heavenly harvest from that field,
Nor tares permit to sow,
Nor hate, nor woe
In the pure soil God's grace itself would sow; —
But bloom and open all the day
And be a flower that none shall pluck away,
A rose of Fruitland's quiet dell,
A child intent on doing well
Devout secluded from all sin
Fragrance without and fair within
A plant matured in God's device
An Amaranth in Paradise.

Monday, 17 July, 1843.

This morning, not feeling well, I did not join the singing class, but kept my bed till after breakfast. We had no lessons to-day and I sewed. I believe I will write a story called The May Morning.

A FABLE

The May Morning

Early one morning in May a father conducted his son Theodore into the garden of a rich man which the boy had never yet seen. The garden was situated at a distance from the city, and it was adorned with all sorts of shrubs and plants, beds of flowers and fruit trees, shady alleys and pleasant groves. Through the middle of the garden wandered a pellucid stream which fell from a rock and formed a large pool at its foot. In the cool dell the water turned a mill. In the most beautiful spot in the garden were seats entwined with roses and verdant bowers.

Theodore could not satiate his eyes with the charms of the place. He walked beside his father mostly in silent amaze, but sometimes he would exclaim: "O Father, how lovely and beautiful is this garden!"

When they had seen many things and were weary with their walk the father conducted the boy through the plantations to the fall of a stream and they sat down on the brow of a hill. Here they listened to the roaring of the water which tumbled foaming from the ledge of the rocks, and in the surrounding thickets were perched nightingales which mingled their strains with the hoarse murmur of the fall. And Theodore thought he never yet had heard nightingales sing so delightfully. While they thus sat and listened they heard the voice of a man and the voices of children. They were the children of the miller, a boy and a girl, and they were leading their old blind grandfather between them, and telling him about the beautiful shrubs and flowers by the wayside, and amusing the old man by their lively and simple prattle.

They conducted him to a seat in an arbor and kissed him, and ran about the garden to gather flowers and fruit for him. But the old man smiled, and when he was alone he uncovered his head and prayed with a cheerful countenance. Then the hearts of Theodore and his father overflowed, and they offered up prayer and praise with the old man, and Theodore was overcome by his feelings so that he could not repress his tears.

The children soon afterwards appeared, and they shouted from afar, and they brought sweet-smelling flowers and ripe fruit to their blind grandfather. But Theodore said to his father as they were returning home, "O what a delightful, what a happy morning!"

THE FOUNTAIN

"The little fountain flows
So noiseless through the wood
The wanderer tastes repose
And from its silent flood
Learns meekly to do good."

It's short, but I thought it was very pretty.

Tuesday, 18.

This morning after doing my work I had lessons. I wrote some in my journal and did some sums. In the afternoon I went blue-berrying with Lizzie and picked nearly, if not quite, a quart. I read in the evening.

Wednesday, 19.

We had a descriptive lesson this morning and each of us wrote a description of Fruitlands. I wrote the following one: —

The Community Settle

"Fruitlands"

It is a beautiful place surrounded by hills, green fields and woods, and Still River is at some distance flowing quietly along. Wachusett and Monadoc Mountains are in sight, and also some houses and fields of grain. The house itself is now very pleasantly situated. It has a vegetable garden behind it and some fruit trees. On the left a hill on the top of which are pastures and a road. In front is a small garden, and fields and a house at some distance. On the right is a large barn, grain and potato field, woods and mountains. There are many pleasant walks about Fruitlands, and berry fields, though the berries are not yet quite ripe.

It is a pleasant place to live in, I think.

Thursday, 20.

I had my lesson this morning with Mr. Lane and I did some sums with fractions. I never did any till Mr. Lane began to teach me, and I think I have learned more lately than I ever did before. I think I understand what I learn too. In the afternoon I had my shower bath and sewed. Mrs. Lovejoy came here to see Mother and brought her little baby with her. I took care of it a good deal. Charlotte and Ellen Dudley came to see me and went to Mrs. Barnard's of an errand with me. I there became acquainted with Adelaide Barnard. We all went into the schoolhouse and played together. In the evening I sewed a little bit and then went to bed.

Sunday, 23.

I did not feel well this morning, so I did not attend the readings, but read in Miss Edgeworth's "Belinda." In the afternoon I sewed some and mother finished "Sowing and Reaping" aloud. I then went to look for blueberries, but did not find but a very few. When I returned I had supper and after that I read.

Monday, 24.

I had no lessons to-day, Mr. Lane being unwell and father busy. Mother washed and Louisa and I helped her. I then shelled some peas for dinner. Yesterday Christy went away. He will return sometime I guess. In the afternoon I read part of "Mademoiselle Panache." I then wrote my journal and took care of Abba. William and I then ironed till we went to supper. In the evening I looked for berries and went pretty early to bed.

Tuesday, 25.

This morning I had lessons by myself. I did a French lesson and wrote in my journal. I then sewed some. In the afternoon I made some little presents to give Abba as to-morrow is her birthday. I then raked hay. In the evening I read in "Motherless Ellen."

Wednesday, 26.

Abba's birthday. We did not do anything to celebrate except that I put some presents into her stocking last night and she found them there this morning. After breakfast father and Mr. Lane started for Boston with Mr. Hecker. We had no lessons. I washed, and the three other children went to a mill for a walk. I arranged a room for myself. It is to be my room and I to stay by myself in it. I then set the dinner table. The children did not return till after dinner. I had a bath and then arranged some pictures for my scrap-book. As Mother was going into the fields to help with the hay, I joined her, and after working there some time went with Louisa to look for berries. We found about a pint. In the evening I read in "Motherless Ellen" some more.

I rose pretty early this morning and having bathed and dressed sat down to write my journal. Having done so I went downstairs and eat breakfast. After I had done I went with Louisa and William to pick blackberries. We got about two quarts. When we returned I read and then worked with William. In the afternoon I wrote and went to Mrs. Lovejoy's. I then had a bath and wrote, after which I read in the newspapers. In the evening I played.

POETRY

I never cast a flower away
The gift of one who cared for me
A little flower — a faded flower
But it was done reluctantly.

I never looked a last adieu
To things familiar but my heart
Shrank with a feeling almost pain
Even from their lifelessness.

I never spoke the word farewell
But with an utterance faint and broken
A heart with yearning for the time
When it should never more be spoken.

September, 6.

I think the world would be a very dismal world without books. I could not live without them. I take so much pleasure in reading beautiful stories and poetry. I like to hear beautiful words and thoughts. Beautiful is my favorite word. If I like anything I always say it is beautiful. It is a beautiful word. I can't tell the color of it. Louisa and I took a walk. It was pleasant if it had only been a little warmer. When we returned we sat in our chamber. I wrote down all the beautiful names we could think of, and in the evening wrote the colors of them.

[Here Anna's journal written at Fruitlands comes to a sudden ending. Numberless pages have been torn out carefully, and Mr. Alcott's handwriting appears in footnotes here and there, showing that it was he who destroyed the story of the later days of Fruitlands written from his youthful daughter's pen. It is one more proof of the intensity of his feelings regarding Fruitlands, and the bitter disappointment that Time never softened. His own journal written there has also been destroyed. It seems as if that experience of failure was too heartrending to him to allow the world to share it. We only get glimpses here and there with which to construct a picture of the New Eden where these Transcendentalists worked out a beloved theory and found it wanting. We have the account of the start, so full of enthusiasm and ecstatic hopefulness. The curtain has been drawn over the rest as carefully as was possible. Her journal starts again in 1846, but it does not state the month. In it she mentions a point which reveals something of Mr. Alcott's philosophy. She says: "Father said that if a person wanted a thing very much and thought of it a great deal, that they would probably have it."]

Where Abba May's Stocking was hung the night before her birthday
Anna's bedroom is on the right, next to Mrs. Alcott's. The portraits of the "Little Women" hang on the wall.

VIII - Louisa May Alcott's Diary at Fruitlands

[1]

September 1st. — I rose at five and had my bath. I love cold water! Then we had our singing-lesson with Mr. Lane. After breakfast I washed dishes, and ran on the hill till nine and had some thoughts, — it was so beautiful up there. Did my lessons, — wrote and spelt and did sums; and Mr. Lane read a story, "The Judicious Father." How a rich girl told a poor girl not to look over the fence at the flowers, and was cross to her because she was unhappy. The Father heard her do it, and made the girls change clothes. The poor one was glad to do it, and he told her to keep them. But the rich one was very sad; for she had to wear the old ones a week, and after that she was good to shabby girls. I liked it very much, and I shall be kind to poor people.

Father asked us what was God's noblest work. Anna said *men,* but I said *babies.* Men are often bad; babies never are. We had a long talk, and I felt better after it, and *cleared up.*

We had bread and fruit for dinner. I read and walked and played till supper-time. We sung in the evening. As I went to bed the moon came up very brightly and looked at me. I felt sad because I have been cross to-day, and did not mind Mother. I cried, and then I felt better, and said that piece from Mrs. Sigourney, "I must not tease my mother." I get to sleep saying poetry, — I know a great deal.

Thursday, 14th. — Mr. Parker Pillsbury came, and we talked about the poor slaves. I had a music lesson with Miss P. I hate her, she is so fussy. I ran in the wind and played be a horse, and had a lovely time in the woods with Anna and Lizzie. We were fairies, and made gowns and paper wings. I "flied" the highest of all. In the evening they talked about travelling. I thought about Father going to England, and said this piece of poetry I found in Byron's poems:

> "When I left thy shores, O Naxos,
>   Not a tear in sorrow fell;
> Not a sigh or faltered accent
>   Told my bosom's struggling swell."

It rained when I went to bed and made a pretty noise on the roof.

Sunday, 24th. — Father and Mr. Lane have gone to N. H. to preach. It was very lovely...Anna and I got supper. In the eve I read "Vicar of Wakefield." I was cross to-day, and I cried when I went to bed. I made good resolutions, and felt better in my heart. If I only *kept* all I make, I should be the best girl in the world. But I don't, and so am very bad.

(Poor little sinner! She says the same at fifty. — L. M. A.)

October 8th. — When I woke up, the first thought I got was, "It's Mother's birthday: I must be very good." I ran and wished her a happy birthday, and gave her my kiss. After breakfast we gave her our presents. I had a moss cross and a piece of poetry for her.

We did not have any school, and played in the woods and got red leaves. In the evening we danced and sung, and I read a story about "Contentment." I wish I was rich, I was good, and we were all a happy family this day.

We sang the following song:

SONG OF MAY

> Hail, all hail, thou merry month of May,
> We will hasten to the woods away
> Among the flowers so sweet and gay,
> Then away to hail the merry merry May —
>   The merry merry May —

Then away to hail the merry merry month of May.

Hark, hark, hark, to hail the month of May,
How the songsters warble on the spray,
And we will be as blith as they,
Then away to hail the merry merry May —
Then away to hail the merry merry month of May.

I think this is a very pretty song and we sing it a good deal.

Thursday, 12th. — After lessons I ironed. We all went to the bam and husked com. It was good fun. We worked till eight o'clock and had lamps. Mr. Russell came. Mother and Lizzie are going to Boston. I shall be very lonely without dear little Betty, and no one will be as good to me as Mother. I read in Plutarch. I made a verse about sunset: —

"Softly doth the sun descend
  To his couch behind the hill,
Then, oh, then, I love to sit
  On mossy banks beside the rill."

Anna thought it was very fine; but I didn't like it very well.

Friday, Nov. 2nd. — Anna and I did the work. In the evening Mr. Lane asked us, "What is man?" These were our answers: A human being; an animal with a mind; a creature; a body; a soul and a mind. After a long talk we went to bed very tired.

(No wonder, after doing the work and worrying their little wits with such lessons. — L. M. A.)

A sample of the vegetarian wafers used at Fruitlands: —

Vegetable diet and sweet repose. Animal food and nightmare.
Pluck your body from the orchard; do not snatch it from the shamble.
Without flesh diet there could be no blood-shedding war.
Apollo eats no flesh and has no beard; his voice is melody itself.
Snuff is no less snuff though accepted from a gold box.

Tuesday, 20th. — I rose at five, and after breakfast washed the dishes, and then helped mother work. Miss P. is gone, and Anna in Boston with Cousin Louisa. I took care of Abba (May) in the afternoon. In the evening I made some pretty things for my dolly. Father and Mr. L. had a talk, and father asked us if *we* saw any reason for us to separate. Mother wanted to, she is so tired. I like it, but not the school part or Mr. L.

Eleven years old. Thursday, 29th. — It was Father's and my birthday. We had some nice presents. We played in the snow before school. Mother read "Rosamond" when we sewed. Father asked us in the eve what fault troubled us most. I said my bad temper.

I told mother I liked to have her write in my book. She said she would put in more, and she wrote this to help me: —

"Dear Louey, — Your handwriting improves very fast. Take pains and do not be in a hurry. I like to have you make observations about our conversations and your own thoughts. It helps you to express them and to understand your little self. Remember, dear girl, that a diary should be an epitome of your life. May it be a record of pure thought and good actions, then you will indeed be the precious child of your loving mother."

December 10th. — I did my lessons, and walked in the afternoon. Father read to us in dear "Pilgrim's Progress." Mr. L. was in Boston and we were glad. In the eve father and mother and Anna and I had a long talk. I was very unhappy, and we all cried. Anna and I cried in bed, and I prayed God to keep us all together.

[1] When she was ten years old.

IX - Autumn Disappointment

As any one knows who has any experience in farming, the true farmer spirit shows itself in the man who accepts the disappointment of a meagre crop in spite of his dreams of a plentiful harvest, and working diligently, gets what he can from it.

The crops at Fruitlands underwent many vicissitudes. No sooner did a crop show some sort of promise than they turned it back into the earth again, in order to enrich the soil, they said. This method did not tend to fill the winter storehouse with the needed vegetables, and a faint suggestion of disillusionment began to creep into the perfect harmony of the consociate family as autumn approached. Early in September Mr. Alcott and Charles Lane went on a trip in search of recruits. They went to Providence and had an evening's conversation with Mrs. Newcomb and some of her friends, during which Mr. Alcott said that, as competition had made facilities so great, they might take that opportunity to go on to New York. Charles Lane then spoke up and said there was no other objection than lack of means, whereupon the company contributed the necessary amount. In writing to Oldham about it, Charles Lane passes comment on what he saw: "We went to the Graham House to breakfast where we found some people half if not quite alive" and again: "The number of living persons in the 300,000 inhabitants of New York is very small." During this visit they went to see Mrs. L. M. Child, who gave the following account of it:

"A day or two after [Theodore] Parker left, Alcott and Lane called to see me. I asked, 'What brings you to New York?' 'I don't know,' said Mr. Alcott; 'it seems a miracle that we are here.' Mr. Child and John Hopper went to hear a discussion between them and W. H. Channing. I asked Mr. Child what they talked about. 'Lane divided man into three states, — the disconscious, the conscious, and the unconscious. The disconscious is the state of the pig; the conscious is the baptism by water; and the unconscious is the baptism by fire.' I laughed, and said, 'Well, how did the whole discussion affect your mind?' 'Why, after I heard them talk a few minutes, I'll be cursed if I knew whether I had any mind at all.' J. H. stayed rather longer, though he left in the midst. He said they talked about mind and body. 'What did they say?' 'Why, Channing seemed to think there was some connection between mind and body; but those Boston folks, so far as I could understand 'em, seemed to think the body was all sham!'"

There is a story that on their return from New York they went by steamer to New Haven. All the money that had been contributed by Mrs. Newcomb and her friends had gone, but that did not trouble the philosophers. They boarded the boat quite serenely and when it started sat on deck enjoying the breeze. The ticket-man came to each passenger for his ticket, and when he came to Mr. Alcott and Mr. Lane, sitting there in their linen suits, he asked them for theirs. Quite undisturbed Mr. Alcott replied that they had no money or scrip, but they would quite willingly pay their way by addressing the passengers and crew with a little conversation in the saloon. It is said that in reply the language of the ticket-man was not as civil as it should have been.

It was all very pleasant, this wandering off and showing their linen tunics to the world and holding conversations to enlighten people in regard to the future wonders of the New Eden, but the day they left Fruitlands Joseph Palmer was off attending to his cattle at No Town, and the crop of barley had been cut and was waiting to be harvested. Poor Mrs. Alcott looked at it with anxious eyes. The granary was almost empty and this barley meant food. She could forget herself, but she could not ignore the needs of her children. Christopher Greene and Larned and Bower were also away. The barley lay there with no one to bring it in to a safe shelter. The next day she looked at it again with a sinking heart. As the afternoon waned, black clouds covered the sky and flashes of lightning rent seams through them with terrifying rapidity. Then Mrs. Alcott made a quick decision. Gathering all the baskets she could find, she carried them to the barley-field with the help of the children, and in hot haste they gathered the barley into the baskets and dragged them to the granary, and then ran back as fast as they could for more. Thus they worked with all their strength, and when the storm broke, they had saved enough to last them for at least a few weeks.

So if Mrs. Alcott lacked, as Lane said, spiritual insight, she fortunately for them had practical foresight, from which they all reaped a benefit.

The following letter to Mr. Oldham is suggestive of the trend of affairs in the community: —

The Outer Kitchen

Fruitlands, Harvard, Mass.
September 29, 1843.

On our arrival at home we learnt that in our absence several friends and strangers had called, amongst them S. Bower, Parker Pillsbury, and an acquaintance, Mr. Hamond of New Ipswich in New Hampshire State. Thinking the latter worth seeing we went to visit him, a distance of about twenty-five miles. He is married to an exoteric wife of some good household qualities; he has built with his own hands a smart cottage, being an expert workman, and has moreover a respectable talent for portrait painting which he estimates humbly without a consciousness of humility. Next to Edward Palmer, he is a person who, I should think, would make one with us. He introduced us at two houses to four females who vitally considered constitute with himself the whole of the town. Our visit there will do some good, for though they have read my letters printed last winter in the newspapers, yet the presence of a living person is much more real a thing. I saw their good intentions were greatly encouraged. I could not dissuade the oldest from promising never to taste flesh again, which I was rather inclined to on account of her years...

On Saturday last Anna Alcott most magnanimously walked her little legs fourteen miles in about five hours down to old Concord, where our friends appear to have been pretty somnolent since our departure. On Tuesday we returned on foot, and accomplished somewhat towards the liberation of the animals by a heroine of thirteen. Mr. Emerson is, I think, quite stationary: he is off the Railroad of Progress, and merely an elegant, kindly observer of all who pass onwards, and notes down their aspect while they remain in sight; of course, when they arrive at a new station they are gone from and for him. I see Mr. John Sterling dedicates his new tragedy of "Strafford" to him: no very alarming honor! I suppose that Thomas Carlyle, with all his famous talking, does not yet *actually* lead the people out of their troubles. These worthy and enlightened scribblers will do little to save the nation. Some there are I hope of more real solid metal...

Samuel Bower has not yet had your note, as I am not sure where he is. He could not, it seems, long endure Joseph Palmer's offer of land, etc., it was so solitary. He called here when we were on our long journey on his way to Lowell, the Manchester of New England. If his aims are high and his head clear, or his hands effective, he will not be able to wander far from us; but a wanderer it is certain he must be allowed to be. Abraham [Abram Everett] comes and goes with some regard to the law within him; he is now busy with our latter hay, the maize, buckwheat, etc.

What is to be our destiny I can in no wise guess. Mr. Alcott makes such high requirements of all persons that few are likely to stay, even of his own family, unless he can become more tolerant of defect. He is an artist in human character requiring every painter to be a Michael Angelo. He also does not wish to keep a hospital, nor even a school, but to be surrounded by Masters — Masters of Art, of the one grand Art of human life. I suppose such a standard would soon empty your Concordium as well as every other house, which I suppose you call by insinuation "Discordiums," or, more elegantly, "Discordia." I propose to pass at least another winter in New England to know more averagingly what they are, as the last was particularly severe. I have gone about on these several journeys in the simple tunic and linen garments and mean to keep them on as long as I can. We have had a fine summer of three months, and a fine autumn seems on hand. Sharp frost this morning, yet we took our bath as usual out-of-doors in the gray of the morn at one-half past five. Health, the grand external condition, still attends me, every stranger rating me ten or twelve years younger than I am; so that if such are the effects of climate I may indeed be happy, for my youthfulness is not all appearance — I *feel* as buoyant and as boyish as I look, which I find a capital endorsement to my assertions about diet, etc. It staggers the sceptical and sets their selfish thoughts to work...

Hoping that all minds are thus laboring, let us, my dear friend, act as if all good progress depended upon us and unfailingly present a clean breast to Eternal Love, shedding forth our full measure in the clearest Light; in which I am

Thine truly,
Chas. Lane.

Abraham just notifies me there is work in the field, so I must go.

Joseph Palmer had offered his old house at No Town to Samuel Bower as a refuge in which to test his theory of the benefits to be derived from accustoming the body to live without the enervating burden of clothing. Bower's experiences in this line at Fruitlands had not been satisfactory or convincing, as it was only at night that he could make the experiment, and then they insisted on his donning a white garment for his peregrinations in the open. Even this caused agitation in the neighborhood, and tales of a white ghost wandering over the hillside caused much alarm, and several times a posse went out from the village to look into the matter. At No Town he could be in solitude. While there he wrote a number of articles for the *Liberator,* in one of which he predicted the full regeneration of man, "if we can rid the kitchen of its horrors and keep our tables free from the mangled corse."

In another letter Lane writes to Oldham: —

...At present I am situated thus. All the persons who have joined us during the summer have from some cause or other quitted, they say in consequence of Mr. Alcott's despotic manner, which he interprets as their not being equal to the Spirit's demands. Joseph Palmer, who has done, and is doing our farm work for love, still remains in the same relation as he ever did.

Palmer says that having once declared this land free we should never go back, at least until the work has been fairly tested. Under all this it should be stated that Mrs. Alcott has no spontaneous inclination towards a larger family than her own natural one, of spiritual ties she knows nothing, though to keep all together she does and would go through a good deal of exterior and interior toil. I hoped I had done with pecuniary affairs, but it seems I am not to be let off. The crops, I believe, will not discharge all the obligations they were expected to liquidate, and against going further into debt I am most determinately settled...You will perceive that I have, like yourself, a small peck of troubles; not quite heavy enough to drive me to a juncture with our friends, the Shakers, but sufficiently so to put the thought into one's head, as you perceive. In the midst of all these events and of William's illness, who is in bed eight or ten days with a sort of bilious fever, I am not without the consolatory hope that some measure of Spirit utilitary is bound up with our obscure doings.

Yours most affectionately,
Charles Lane.

At a late visit on foot to Roxbury, I found the numbers at Brook Farm considerably diminished. I don't know what they will say to my letter if they see it in *The New Age,* but never mind.

From now on clashing of wills disturbed the serenity of Fruitlands. Charles Lane, despondent over the course of events and the sense of failure, and seeing further financial complications in store for him, began seriously to consider the plan of life adopted by the Shakers whose well-filled corn-bins and full-rigged haylofts bespoke a system which provided plenty for man and beast, and gave time for alternate work and meditation. He began to talk of this to Mr. Alcott and urged him toward a more monastic life, and then suggested that they should join them. That he had great influence with Mr. Alcott is evident, and Mrs. Alcott, who fully realized this, grew restless and then alarmed.

In writing to Oldham, Lane kept dwelling upon Mrs. Alcott. Once he wrote: "Mrs. Alcott has passed from the ladylike to the industrious order, but she has much inward experience to realize, Her pride is not yet eradicated and her peculiar maternal love blinds her to all else — whom does it not so blind for a season?" [1]

And he ascribes the failure of other persons to join the experiment largely to Mrs. Alcott, "who vows that her own family are all that she lives for." No such narrow purpose, Lane adds, has inspired him; and he blames Mr. Alcott for listening too much to his family affections, and regarding too much what that guardian angel of middle-class England, Mrs. Grundy, will say.

In speaking of Mr. Alcott, he complains that "constancy to his wife and inconstancy to the Spirit have blurred over his life forever."

Poor Mrs. Alcott, poor "Marmee," as her daughters called her! — in her loyalty she had almost worked her fingers to the bone with no thanks for it. Her days had passed without any help to lighten the manual labor. At first they said that not a lamp could lighten Fruitlands because the oil contained animal fat, and only bayberry candles could be used, and only a few of them. But Mrs. Alcott then rebelled. How could she sew and mend the clothes with such poor light? There seemed some sense in this, so one small lamp was brought to Fruitlands just for her. The philosophers tried sitting in the dark, but one by one would try to find some pretext to join her at the sewing-table, and Mrs. Alcott's lamp burned bright and steady, an emblem of her own true and faithful heart.

Ellery Channing said: "Mrs. Alcott was one of the most refined persons of my acquaintance. She told me years afterwards that in 1843-44 she feared for her husband's sanity; he did such strange things without seeming to know how odd they were; wearing only linen clothes and canvas shoes, and eating only vegetables."

Charles Lane's Room

The old cowhide in which some of the most valuable of the books were shipped from London; also the old chest in which the linen was kept. The spinning-wheel belonged to a former owner.

November 26, 1843, Lane wrote to Oldham from Fruitlands: —

"What with agitations of mind and ills of body, I have passed a less happy time than usual. William was ill a whole month with a low fever so that he could not even sit up in bed for one minute. I had to nurse him while plagued with hands so chapped and sore that I was little more capable than the patient. Then came Mr. [Samuel J.] May's announcement that he should not pay the note to which he had put his hand; so that money affairs and individual property come back again upon me for a season. Thereupon ensued endless discussions, doubts, and anticipations concerning our destiny. These still hang over us. But in the midst of them Mrs. Alcott gives notice that she concedes to the wishes of her friends and shall withdraw to a house which they will provide for herself and her four children. As she will take all the furniture with her, this proceeding necessarily leaves me alone and naked in a new world. Of course Mr. A. and I could not remain together without her. To be 'that devil come from Old England to separate husband and wife,' I will not be, though it might gratify New England to be able to say it. So that you will perceive a separation is possible. Indeed, I believe that under the circumstances it is now inevitable."

Mr. Sanborn says in his "Memoirs of Bronson Alcott": —
"Those who read Louisa's 'Transcendental Wild Oats' will see by her names 'Timon Lion' for Lane, and 'Abel Lamb' for Alcott, that she looked on her father as rather the victim of Lane in the 'Fruitlands' failure. Without conceding this, the impartial observer will say that Lane had the stronger will, and the far more prosaic nature; that he decided most of the questions for his associates in both countries, and that he was rather a hard person to get on with. Neither his first wife, nor Wright, nor Mrs. Alcott, nor Alcott himself, nor the Harvard Shakers, nor finally Oldham, could quite suit him. He over-persuaded Alcott, who was a good farmer and mechanic, to adopt impossible modes of working the 'Fruitlands' farm, and much of their whimsies in dress and food seem to have come from Lane and his English friends. Mrs. Alcott, when reestablished in a home of her own at Concord, early in 1845, offered Lane a home there, and he tried it for a time in the next summer, but still complained, as he had at 'Fruitlands,' that she wished to keep her family small, and made it uncomfortable for guests. Knowing Mrs. Alcott's character well, in the last twenty years of her life, I cannot believe that this was ever true of her. She was hospitality itself, whether poor or rich; and it must have been Lane's own individualism that made him dissatisfied.

"The rigors of a New England winter promoted the dissolution of the 'Fruitlands' Community, but did not alone break it up. A lack of organizing power to control the steady current of selfishness, as well as the unselfish vagaries of his followers, was the real cause. Nothing in fact could be more miserable than the failure of this hopeful experiment."

Mr. Alcott had written in his diary of Emerson: — "It is much to have the vision of the seeing eye. Did most men possess this, the useful hand would be empowered with new dexterity also. Emerson sees me, knows me, and more than all others helps me, — not by noisy praise, not by low appeals to interest and passion, but by turning the eye of others to my stand in reason and the nature of things. Only men of like vision can apprehend and counsel each other. A man whose purpose and act demand but a day or an hour for their completion can do little by way of advising him whose purposes require years for their fulfilment. Only Emerson, of this age, knows me, of all that I have found. Well, every one does not find *one* man, one *very man through and through*. Many are they who live and die alone, known only to their survivors of an after-century."

How he recalled that now! He was tossed in mind and troubled beyond measure. All his beautiful dreams were melting away one by one. Everything seemed to be falling from his grasp. Most of the crops had failed; — the enthusiastic lovers of "The Newness" had proved themselves false and had slipped away as the cold weather approached. All his wonderful plans had come to naught. He had promised to the world the vision of a new Eden: he had believed it could exist: he had worked for it with his whole soul: he had nothing to show for it but failure. Would his friend Emerson stay by him in his anguish? He believed he would, and yet how meet his friend? How face the world?

The cold penetrated the old house. William Lane lay ill in his room and his father watched over him. All were heavy-hearted. It was as late as January that Charles Lane and his son moved to the Shakers. After that Mr. Alcott retired to his room, as he thought, to face the end. Mr. Sanborn tells us: "The final expulsion from this Paradise nearly cost Mr. Alcott his life. He retired to his chamber, refused food, and was on the point of dying from grief and abstinence, when his wife prevailed on him to continue longer in this ungrateful world."

This prayer was written in his diary after leaving Fruitlands: "Light, O source of light! give Thou unto thy servant, sitting in the perplexities of this surrounding darkness. Hold Thou him steady to Thee, to truth, and to himself; and in Thine own due time give him clearly to the work for which Thou art thus slowly preparing him, proving his faith meanwhile in Thyself and in his kind."

"Shall I say with Pestalozzi that I was not made by this world, nor for it, — wherefore am I placed in it if I was found unfit? And the world that found him thus asked not whether it was his fault or that of another; but it bruised him with an iron hammer, as the bricklayer breaks an old brick to fill up a crevice."

"That is failure when a man's idea ruins him, when he is dwarfed and killed by it; but when he is ever growing by it, ever true to it, and does not lose it by any partial or immediate failures, — that is success, whatever it seems to the world."

In speaking of the Fruitlands experiment Mr. Sanborn says: —

"It brought its own compensations, and left the whole Alcott family richer and not poorer for this romantic experience with its sad termination. It prepared Alcott to face more patiently the storms of later life, and to train his daughter, who was his best single gift to the world, better for her conspicuous service. And 'Fruitlands' will be remembered, perhaps longer than most of the adventures that awaited this romantic household in its voyage of life...

The Bedroom
Where Mr. Alcott nearly succumbed to his despair at the failure of his "New Eden"

"There was some foundation for Alcott's despair at 'Fruitlands,' and with the ill success that followed him after the flourishing Temple School in Boston. Emerson, the gentlest and least exacting of men, looking at his friend's situation a few years after the 'Fruitlands' experiment, wrote in his private journal —

"'The plight of Mr. Alcott! The most refined and the most advanced soul we have had in New England; who makes all other souls appear slow and cheap and mechanical; a man of such courtesy and greatness that in conversation all others, even the intellectual, seem sharp, and fighting for I victory and angry, — while he has the unalterable sweetness of a muse! Yet because he cannot earn money by his talk or his pen, or by school-keeping, or bookkeeping, or editing, or any kind of meanness, — nay, for this very cause that he is ahead of his contemporaries, is higher than they, and keeps himself out of the shop condescensions and arts which they stoop to, — or, unhappily, need not stoop to, but find themselves, as it were, born to; therefore it is the unanimous opinion of New England judges that this man must die! We do not adjudge him to hemlock or garroting, — we are much too hypocritical and cowardly for that. But we not less surely doom him by refusing to protest against this doom, or combine to save him, and to set him in employments fit for him and salutary for the State.'"

The poem written by Mr. Alcott, with the title "The Return," may fittingly close this chapter: —

"As from himself he fled
   Outcast, insane,
Tormenting demons drove him from the gate:
   Away he sped,
   Casting his joys behind,
   His better mind:

Recovered,
Himself again,
Over his threshold led,
Peace fills his breast,
He finds rest,
Expecting angels his arrival wait."

[1] Sanborn's *Bronson Alcott*.

X - In After Years

More than thirty years after the Fruitlands failure, Mrs. Caroline Sherman, of Chicago, heard from Mr. Alcott its story as he came to view it in later years. She says: —
"One day at Concord Mr. Alcott consented to give his experience at Fruitlands, and for two hours he entertained the little company with the happiest of humor, as he told the story of his effort to realize an ideal community. Together with Charles Lane, he purchased a location on the north side of a sandy hill in Harvard, and started out with the idea of welcoming hospitably to their community any human being who sought admission. Mr. Alcott described the various sorts of quaint characters who came to live with them, lured by the charms of Utopia and Arcadia combined. Only a vegetable diet was allowed; for the rights of animals to life, liberty, and the pursuit of happiness formed a fundamental principle in their constitution. This not only cut

them off from beef, but from milk and eggs. The milk belonged to the calf, and the chicken had a right to its existence as well as the infant. Even the canker-worms that infested the apple trees were not to be molested. They had as much right to the apples as man had. Unfortunately farm operations were not started until well into June, and the only crop raised that was of value as dependence was barley; but the philosophers did not flinch at the thought of an exclusively barley diet. Now and then they gave a thought as to what they should do for shoes when those they now had were gone; for depriving the cow of her skin was a crime not to be tolerated. The barley crop was injured in harvesting, and before long actual want was staring them in the face. This burden fell heaviest upon Mrs. Alcott, for, as housewife, it was her duty to prepare three meals a day. They remained at Fruitlands till midwinter in dire poverty, all the guests having taken their departure as provisions vanished. Friends came to the rescue, and, concluded Mr. Alcott, with a tone of pathos in his voice: 'We put our four little women on an ox-sled, [1] and made our way to Concord. So faded one of the dreams of my youth. I have given you the facts as they were; Louisa has given the comic side in "Transcendental Wild Oats"; but Mrs. Alcott could give you the tragic side.'"

The odes addressed to Alcott by Thoreau and Lowell should be recalled in connection with these reminiscences of his later years: —

THE HILLSIDE HOUSE

BY HENRY DAVID THOREAU

Here Alcott thought, — respect a wise man's door!
   No kinder heart a mortal form e'er held;
Its easy hinges ope forevermore
   At touch of all, — or fervid Youth or Eld.

A mounting sage was he, and could essay
   Bold flights of hope, that softly fed his tongue
With honey; then flew swift that happy day.
   As tranced in joy on his pure themes we hung.

He knew the Scholar's art; with insight spent
   On Plato's sentence, that best poesy,
And calm philosophy, his soul intent
   Cleared the grey film of Earth and Air and Sea.

He might have lapsed, — but Heaven him held along, —
   Or splendrous faded like some sunset dream;
But long shall live! though this bare, humble song
   Gains not his dignity, — nor rounds its theme.

He'll dwell (doubt not) in that fond, wished-for Land,
   Where the broad Concave's stars unquailing bloom;

The guest of angels, that consolers stand, —
    Sweetly forgot in light Earth's lowly tomb.

Then may I wait, dear Alcott, of thy court,
    Or bear a mace in thy Platonic reign!
Though sweet Philosophy be not my forte.
    Nor Mincio's reed, nor Learning's weary gain.

ODE TO ALCOTT [2]

BY JAMES RUSSELL LOWELL

Hear him but speak, and you will feel
    The shadows of the Portico
Over your tranquil spirit steal,
    To modulate all joy and woe
    To one subdued, subduing glow;
Above our squabbling business hours,
Like Phidian Jove's, his beauty lowers,
His nature satirizes ours;
    A form and front of Attic grace,
    He shames the higgling market-place,
And dwarfs our more mechanic powers.

What throbbing verse can fitly render
That face so pure, so trembling-tender?
    Sensation glimmers through its rest,
It speaks unmanacled by words,
    As full of motion as a nest
That palpitates with unfledged birds;
    'Tis likest to Bethesda's stream.
Forewarned through all its thrilling springs,
    White with the angel's coming gleam,
And rippled with his fanning wings.

- - - - - - - - - - - -

Himself unshaken as the sky,
His words, like whirlwinds, spin on high
    Systems and creeds pellmell together;
'Tis strange as to a deaf man's eye,
While trees uprooted splinter by.
    The dumb turmoil of stormy weather;
    Less of iconoclast than shaper,
His spirit, safe behind the reach
Of the tornado of his speech,
    Burns calmly as a glowworm's taper.

As Mr. Alcott suffered acutely from the disastrous ending of the Fruitlands Community, so also did Charles Lane. The cherished ideal of the regeneration of the world by a vivid example was shattered beyond repair. Saddened and disillusioned he returned to Alcott House in England.

In writing to Thoreau from London, in 1848, Emerson gives a description of him. He says: "I went last Sunday for the first time to see Lane at Ham, and dined with him. He was full of friendliness and hospitality; has a school of sixteen children, one lady as matron, then Oldham. This is all the household. They looked just comfortable." The matron here spoken of was undoubtedly a Miss Hannah Bond, who had lived at Owen's Community at Harmony Hall, and in due time Lane cast aside his antagonism to family ties and married her. But from his letters to Joseph Palmer, it is evident that his experience in life never allowed him freedom from questions of money and property. He had sunk his all in the experiment at Fruitlands, as "an offering to the Eternal Spirit." One feels a note of bitterness in him from a letter written by Wright to Oldham in which he says: "I have been told that Mr. Lane says Alcott is an unpractical dreamer, or something tantamount thereto. Alas! how far shall we have to go to find those who will deliver the same opinion of C. L. [Charles Lane] and W. O. [William Oldham] and others whom I could mention! Sometimes I almost suspect that of myself. The world has decided pretty truly. I begin to respect its decision and to suspect my own."

And from the following paragraph the pain and disheartenment of a disappointed life shows itself with infinite pathos, as Wright says: "Somehow or other I seem to have made up my mind that it is for me to die, to which I look forward with hope rather than terror." "What have I ever done?" he asks, and responds bitterly, "Nothing, absolutely nothing! I have dreamed only of great deeds. Let me never attempt again what is beyond my being's power."

Fruitlands was left in the hands of Joseph Palmer, who bought it of Charles Lane. The latter, fully aware of the shrewd common sense that lurked beneath an eccentric exterior, urged Joseph Palmer to join him in founding a larger Community, connecting a farm in Leominster with that of Fruitlands as a plant on which to work out a scheme that would promise some measure of success. They drew up the following paper and it was duly signed and sealed: —

Whereas it is desireable to form Associations of well disposed persons for the supply of their physical and mental requirements, for the support of a free school for youth, and a home for the aged, destitute and indigent, and Whereas a capital of one hundred dollars for each associate is deemed sufficient for beginning such an Association, We, the undersigned do agree to the purchase of estates in Leominster and Harvard, Massachusetts, for the purpose of forming such an Association which we propose to commence on the first of January next, to the amount of five thousand dollars capital, afterwards to be extended by the addition of new shares for the purchase of more real estate at the discretion of the shareholders assembled on the first Monday in January in each year, so that all persons interested shall hold equal rights by possessing one share only. The property now in hand for this purpose consists of Land and Buildings in Leominster and Harvard, together about 190 acres with Stock, Tools, Provisions, etc., needful for carrying out the said design held in the name of Joseph Palmer.

Joseph Palmer.
Charles Lane,

August 18, 1846.

But this same shrewd common sense evidently stood in the way of bringing this plan into actual existence, for Charles Lane writes a letter complaining that so much time has been wasted in considering it that he can no longer remain in America, and he sails for England leaving his son William with the Shakers. It is a noticeable proof of the confidence the members of the Community placed in Joseph Palmer that not only Charles Lane wanted him as an associate, but also Samuel Bower, who urged him to join him in founding a Community in a more temperate climate where he could carry out his convictions regarding the casting aside of all outer clothing. But Palmer had seen enough of the Transcendentalists to make him realize the advantages of running his own Community, which he did for upwards of twenty years in a strange, haphazard sort of fashion. He had no name for it, and he never sought recruits, but he never closed his door to the wayfarer, and two large iron pots, one full of baked beans, and the other full of potatoes, stood always ready for the poor and hungry. And so in a humble way, Joseph and Nancy Palmer carried out some of the ideals started at Fruitlands by the Transcendentalists. Calvin Warner lived there off and on for many years, and old Widow Webber sought refuge there, and many came and went. The Harvard people called it a home for tramps and called him "Old Jew Palmer"; but any one who takes the trouble to look closely into his life finds in him a stalwart character full of fibre and unswerving courage, with a very real and abiding religious faith.

He was a fighter for his rights, to the end. The right of way belonging to Fruitlands crossed old Silas Dudley's land to the highway. A continuous battle raged concerning that right of way, and so fierce did it become that when after a heavy snowstorm Joseph Palmer started to shovel the snow off of it, old Silas Dudley shovelled it back again. They kept at it there all day, both irate old men holding out with a grim determination to win. As neither succeeded in gaining advantage, they sent for Mr. Emerson to come and settle the question, which he did.

Quaint old times, quaint old people, — we are grateful for just such pictures of the past!

The following letters were found by a grandson of Joseph Palmer among some old papers at Fruitlands.

New York, Sept. 10, 1846.

To Joseph Palmer,
   Still River,
       Harvard, Mass,

Dear Friend: —

I owe you a severe scolding, and as I always endeavor to pay my debts, here goes. You detained me so long that my school is broken up, the weeds are shoulder high at the door, and my utility in this direction is at an end. Hereafter do not be so dilatory. The good you desire to do will forever escape undone if you are so very, very, very cautious. Yet I am not for haste or for a magnificent work. But having really made your decision and concluded your plan, carry it out faithfully and confidingly on such a scale as you know you can stand by.

I read the Prospectus to several, and none objected. If your Leominster friends have any truth in them, now it will be known. I have written to D. Mack, and have tried to interest some others, and I really think if you could keep me in New England the next winter, the foundation of a rational, soulful, simple Association might be laid. If you had not kept me so long, this might have been possible, but now it seems to be my destiny to obey the manifold and unceasing calls of the Spirit through William Oldham, and return to Alcott House, where your letters will find me, and I hope you will take time to write me all interesting particulars. Perhaps I may work better on that side. At all events, I can assure you I shall continue to take as deep, as active, and as direct an interest in the Leominster and Harvard Association as if I were present. Now that matters are arranged a little more suitably to my nature, I shall work for it with greater freedom and potency. We should help all men out of their false positions, whatever they are, as fast as we can.

Please do not fail to see Edmund Hosmer, and commune freely with friend Emerson. Give my kind remembrances to your wife and daughter, to Mr. Holman, to Thomas and his wife, to Calvin, and all the faithful hearts in your circle. I shall endeavor to write a little history of Fruitlands, past and future, so pray supply me with all the facts as they arise. I hope there will be plenty of good names to put in my book.

I have faith that I shall see you again, but when I cannot guess. Before that time I trust a faithful band will be congregated. I do not care how few, if they be but good and true. Have your son and daughter signed the Prospectus? Mack may come next to make the casting vote, or some other one on whom you could rely.

I know that you and I, S. Ford, and your daughter could carry the design through, if we should have the happiness to be thrown together. God knows and disposes, and blesses all the earnest, in which company may you ever be found with

                    Your resigned brother,
                    Charles Lane.

You have given William his letter, I suppose. See him as often and cheer him as much as you can.

Plenty of people from Brook Farm in consequence of the changes there would be glad to come. The industrials are all obliged to leave. They apply to the N. A. Phalanx, but there is no room for them. Let your plan be known and the house may be filled.

I believe I shall sail in the Diadem for Liverpool in a day or two.

At Mr. Moore's, Knowles Place, Davidson Street, East Merrimack Street, Lowell,
Nov. 6, 1849.

Friend Palmer, —

Having removed to reside in Lowell it may be well to inform you of the change. Perhaps you sometimes come so far in this direction — if so it would be cause of regret to me not to see you. Now, of course, I *shall* see you if you visit L. whilst I locate in it.

Since conversing with you I have meditated much on the great step in progress which I am incessantly reminded it is my interest and duty to make. But how make it? When? Where? and with whom? or, whether alone? On this subject so important to me, to you and to society, I have many new facts and estimates of facts all tending to induce, I trust, early and beneficial action. How far you might be disposed to coincide with me I know not, nor how far your long experience might modify my intentions if communicated. I should certainly like to confer with you at length and without reservation. For such a purpose writing is quite inadequate, so I shall not attempt any statement of my views, etc., herein. One thing, however, I may say, which is that I am fully and I believe finally fixed in the conviction that no Association of persons can be brought to inhabit Fruitlands or your place at Leominster founding itself on those bases and conditions which six years ago were so frequently discussed by us. Be sure C. Lane can send you nobody from England, and I am unaware that there is in this country any one Realist enough to *proceed with the natural economies far enough to satisfy your just expectations.*

I shall most assuredly, if the Infinite Spirit wills, make my home in the open heavens and resume the right so long in abeyance of being naturally and therefore well and sufficiently clothed. The true question is a proper Individualism and nothing that is good and desirable in Socialism can come but after this. This is universally and ethically incontrovertible and physically the solution waits our action. You have long stood on the threshold and best know whether you are prepared now to pass over it and give up your localized and civilized life. I think I am quite clear that it will be necessary to stand within circumstances having less pressure. Suitable natural conditions are indispensable and are to be provided at whatever cost of relinquishment of current enjoyments.

        Yours faithfully,

Saml. Bower.

London, Sept. 29, 1849.

To Joseph Palmer,
    Still River,
        Harvard, Mass.

Dear Friend Palmer: —

If there was a possibility of sending me here only six or seven acres of our old Fruitlands, you should hear no more of me as a claimant.

As this cannot be, and I am once more adrift in consequence of the lease of our house and grounds having been sold, I hope you will have prosperity enough in the culture to release yourself gradually from my encumbrance whereby I may be enabled just to pay the rent on an acre or two to cultivate with my own hands.

Do not let me ask in vain for a good long letter narrating all your local news since I left your hill regions. Mr. Emerson will inform you of William's movements and convey any letters or messages to me. I suppose Dr. Thomas has made a pretty handsome fortune by this time in setting people's mouths in tune and that he will retire to Fruitlands to make sure of it.

Yours faithfully,

Charles Lane

London, Sept. 16, 1851.

To Dr. Thomas Palmer,
    Fitchburg, Mass.

Dear Friend: —

As I am not so certain of reaching your father through the post-office as you, I enclose this note to say that I should feel obliged if you would have the goodness to discharge my claim. Some two or three years have passed since I thought I should no more trouble Mr. Emerson on the subject, which is one among the reasons for urging a settlement. Your business I am sure has been too successful to make it needful to go out of the family for the cash, or at all events for much of it. The farm has been prosperous, and though your father does not aim at commercial profits, yet his industry and integrity bring them to him. I feel it is but as yesterday I and your father went from Harvard to Fitchburg with the cattle. Oh, how hot! I am differently employed now, but I still desire the field and the garden. If I had such a spot here as Fruitlands I should not quit it, but enjoy a life fruitful in all good. Pray, in this matter of the mortgage attend to the request and give my best regards to your father, from whom I should much like to have a letter.

Yours truly,

Charles Lane.

[1] As a matter of fact they did not go to Concord on the ox-sled, but to Still River, where they lived for a year in the house called the "Brick Ends," belonging to the Lovejoy family. They then moved to Concord where Orchard House now stands as a memorial to the later years.

[2] From "Studies for Two Heads."

XI - Transcendental Wild Oats

By Louisa May Alcott

ORIGINAL CHARACTERS OF TRANSCENDENTAL WILD OATS

Timon Lion - Charles Lane.
His Son - William Lane.
Abel Lamb - A. Bronson Alcott.
Sister Hope - Mrs. Alcott.
Her Daughters - The Alcott girls.
John Pease - Samuel Bower.
Forest Absalom - Abram Everett.
Moses White - Joseph Palmer.
Jane Gage - Anna Page.

TRANSCENDENTAL WILD OATS

A CHAPTER FROM AN UNWRITTEN ROMANCE

On the first day of June, 184-, a large wagon, drawn by a small horse and containing a motley load, went lumbering over certain New England hills, with the pleasing accompaniments of wind, rain, and hail. A serene man with a serene child upon his knee was driving, or rather being driven, for the small horse had it all his own way. A brown boy with a William Penn style of countenance sat beside him, firmly embracing a bust of Socrates. Behind them was an energetic-looking woman, with a benevolent brow, satirical mouth, and eyes brimful of hope and courage. A baby reposed upon her lap, a mirror leaned against her knee, and a basket of provisions danced about at her feet, as she struggled with a large, unruly umbrella. Two blue-eyed little girls, with hands full of childish treasures, sat under one old shawl, chatting happily together.

In front of this lively party stalked a tall, sharp-featured man, in a long blue cloak; and a fourth small girl trudged along beside him through the mud as if she rather enjoyed it.

The wind whistled over the bleak hills; the rain fell in a despondent drizzle, and twilight began to fall. But the calm man gazed as tranquilly into the fog as if he beheld a radiant bow of promise spanning the gray sky. The cheery woman tried to cover every one but herself with the big umbrella. The brown boy pillowed his head on the bald pate of Socrates and slumbered peacefully. The little girls sang lullabies to their dolls in soft, maternal murmurs. The sharp-nosed pedestrian marched steadily on, with the blue cloak streaming out behind him like a banner; and the lively infant splashed through the puddles with a ducklike satisfaction pleasant to behold.

Thus these modern pilgrims journeyed hopefully out of the old world, to found a new one in the wilderness.

The editors of *The Transcendental Tripod* had received from Messrs. Lion & Lamb (two of the aforesaid pilgrims) a communication from which the following statement is an extract: —

"We have made arrangements with the proprietor of an estate of about a hundred acres which liberates this tract from human ownership. Here we shall prosecute our effort to initiate a Family in harmony with the primitive instincts of man.

"Ordinary secular farming is not our object. Fruit, grain, pulse, herbs, flax, and other vegetable products, receiving assiduous attention, will afford ample manual occupation, and chaste supplies for the bodily needs. It is intended to adorn the pastures with orchards, and to supersede the labor of cattle by the spade and the pruning-knife.

"Consecrated to human freedom, the land awaits the sober culture of devoted men. Beginning with small pecuniary means, this enterprise must be rooted in a reliance on the succors of an ever-bounteous Providence, whose vital affinities being secured by this union with uncorrupted field and unworldly persons, the caxes and injuries of a life of gain are avoided.

"The inner nature of each member of the Family is at no time neglected. Our plan contemplates all such disciplines, cultures, and habits as evidently conduce to the purifying of the inmates.

"Pledged to the spirit alone, the founders anticipate no hasty or numerous addition to their numbers. The kingdom of peace is entered only through the gates of self-denial; and felicity is the test and the reward of loyalty to the unswerving law of Love."

This prospective Eden at present consisted of an old red farm-house, a dilapidated bam, many acres of meadow-land, and a grove. Ten ancient apple-trees were all the "chaste supply" which the place offered as yet; but, in the firm belief that plenteous orchards were soon to be evoked from their inner consciousness, these sanguine founders had christened their domain Fruitlands.

Here Timon Lion intended to found a colony of Latter Day Saints, who, under his patriarchal sway, should regenerate the world and glorify his name for ever. Here Abel Lamb, with the devoutest faith in the high ideal which was to him a living truth, desired to plant a Paradise, where Beauty, Virtue, Justice, and Love might live happily together, without the possibility of a serpent entering in. And here his wife, unconverted but faithful to the end, hoped, after many wanderings over the face of the earth, to find rest for herself and a home for her children.

"There is our new abode," announced the enthusiast, smiling with a satisfaction quite undamped by the drops dripping from his hat-brim, as they turned at length into a cart-path that wound along a steep hillside into a barren-looking valley.

"A little difficult of access," observed his practical wife, as she endeavored to keep her various household gods from going overboard with every lurch of the laden ark.

"Like all good things. But those who earnestly desire and patiently seek will soon find us," placidly responded the philosopher from the mud, through which he was now endeavoring to pilot the much-enduring horse.

"Truth lies at the bottom of a well, Sister Hope," said Brother Timon, pausing to detach his small comrade from a gate, whereon she was perched for a clearer gaze into futurity.

"That's the reason we so seldom get at it, I suppose," replied Mrs. Hope, making a vain clutch at the mirror, which a sudden jolt sent flying out of her hands.

"We want no false reflections here," said Timon, with a grim smile, as he crunched the fragments under foot in his onward march.

Sister Hope held her peace, and looked wistfully through the mist at her promised home. The old red house with a hospitable glimmer at its windows cheered her eyes; and, considering the weather, was a fitter refuge than the sylvan bowers some of the more ardent souls might have preferred.

The new-comers were welcomed by one of the elect precious, — a regenerate farmer, whose idea of reform consisted chiefly in wearing white cotton raiment and shoes of untanned leather. This costume, with a snowy beard, gave him a venerable, and at the same time a somewhat bridal appearance.

The goods and chattels of the Society not having arrived, the weary family reposed before the fire on blocks of wood, while Brother Moses White regaled them with roasted potatoes, brown bread and water, in two plates, a tin pan, and one mug; his table service being limited. But, having cast the forms and vanities of a depraved world behind them, the elders welcomed hardship with the enthusiasm of new pioneers, and the children heartily enjoyed this foretaste of what they believed was to be a sort of perpetual picnic.

During the progress of this frugal meal, two more brothers appeared. One a dark, melancholy man, clad in homespun, whose peculiar mission was to turn his name hind part before and use as few words as possible. The other was a bland, bearded Englishman, who expected to be saved by eating uncooked food and going without clothes. He had not yet adopted the primitive costume, however; but contented himself with meditatively chewing dry beans out of a basket.

"Every meal should be a sacrament, and the vessels used should be beautiful and symbolical," observed Brother Lamb, mildly, righting the tin pan slipping about on his knees. "I priced a silver service when in town, but it was too costly; so I got some graceful cups and vases of Britannia ware."

"Hardest things in the world to keep bright. Will whiting be allowed in the community?" inquired Sister Hope, with a housewife's interest in labor-saving institutions.

"Such trivial questions will be discussed at a more fitting time," answered Brother Timon, sharply, as he burnt his fingers with a very hot potato. "Neither sugar, molasses, milk, butter, cheese, nor flesh are to be used among us, for nothing is to be admitted which has caused wrong or death to man or beast."

"Our garments are to be linen till we learn to raise our own cotton or some substitute for woollen fabrics," added Brother Abel, blissfully basking in an imaginary future as warm and brilliant as the generous fire before him. A a

"Haou abaout shoes?" asked Brother Moses, surveying his own with interest.

"We must yield that point till we can manufacture an innocent substitute for leather. Bark, wood, or some durable fabric will be invented in time. Meanwhile, those who desire to carry out our idea to the fullest extent can go barefooted," said Lion, who liked extreme measures.

"I never will, nor let my girls," murmured rebellious Sister Hope, under her breath.

"Haou do you cattle'ate to treat the ten-acre lot? Ef things ain't 'tended to right smart, we shan't hev no crops," observed the practical patriarch in cotton.

"We shall spade it," replied Abel, in such perfect good faith that Moses said no more, though he indulged in a shake of the head as he glanced at hands that had held nothing heavier than a pen for years. He was a paternal old soul and regarded the younger men as promising boys on a new sort of lark.

"What shall we do for lamps, if we cannot use any animal substance? I do hope light of some sort is to be thrown upon the enterprise," said Mrs. Lamb, with anxiety, for in those days kerosene and camphene were not, and gas unknown in the wilderness.

"We shall go without till we have discovered some vegetable oil or wax to serve us," replied Brother Timon, in a decided tone, which caused Sister Hope to resolve that her private lamp should be always trimmed, if not burning,

"Each member is to perform the work for which experience, strength, and taste best fit him," continued Dictator Lion. "Thus drudgery and disorder will be avoided and harmony prevail. We shall rise at dawn, begin the day by bathing, followed by music, and then a chaste repast of fruit and bread. Each one finds congenial occupation till the meridian meal; when some deep-searching conversation gives rest to the body and development to the mind. Healthful labor again engages us till the last meal, when we assemble in social communion, prolonged till sunset, when we retire to sweet repose, ready for the next day's activity."

"What part of the work do you incline to yourself?" asked Sister Hope, with a humorous glimmer in her keen eyes.

"I shall wait till it is made clear to me. Being in preference to doing is the great aim, and this comes to us rather by a resigned willingness than a wilful activity, which is a check to all divine growth," responded Brother Timon.

"I thought so." And Mrs. Lamb sighed audibly, for during the year he had spent in her family Brother Timon had so faithfully carried out his idea of "being, not doing," that she had found his "divine growth" both an expensive and unsatisfactory process.

Here her husband struck into the conversation, his face shining with the light and joy of the splendid dreams and high ideals hovering before him.

"In these steps of reform, we do not rely so much on scientific reasoning or physiological skill as on the spirit's dictates. The greater part of man's duty consists in leaving alone much that he now does. Shall I stimulate with tea, coffee, or wine? No. Shall I consume flesh? Not if I value health. Shall I subjugate cattle? Shall I claim property in any created thing? Shall I trade? Shall I adopt a form of religion? Shall I interest myself in politics? To how many of these questions — could we ask them deeply enough and could they be heard as having relation to our eternal welfare — would the response be 'Abstain'?"

A mild snore seemed to echo the last word of Abel's rhapsody, for Brother Moses had succumbed to mundane slumber and sat nodding like a massive ghost. Forest Absalom, the silent man, and John Pease, the English member, now departed to the bam; and Mrs. Lamb led her flock to a temporary fold, leaving the founders of the "Consociate Family" to build castles in the air till the fire went out and the symposium ended in smoke.

The furniture arrived next day, and was soon bestowed; for the principal property of the community consisted in books. To this rare library was devoted the best room in the house, and the few busts and pictures that still survived many flittings were added to beautify the sanctuary, for here the family was to meet for amusement, instruction, and worship.

Any housewife can imagine the emotions of Sister Hope, when she took possession of a large, dilapidated kitchen, containing an old stove and the peculiar stores out of which food was to be evolved for her little family of eleven. Cakes of maple sugar, dried peas and beans, barley and hominy, meal of all sorts, potatoes, and dried fruit. No milk, butter, cheese, tea, or meat appeared. Even salt was considered a useless luxury and spice entirely forbidden by these lovers of Spartan simplicity. A ten years' experience of vegetarian vagaries had been good training for this new freak, and her sense of the ludicrous supported her through many trying scenes.

Unleavened bread, porridge, and water for breakfast; bread, vegetables, and water for dinner; bread, fruit, and water for supper was the bill of fare ordained by the elders. No teapot profaned that sacred stove, no gory steak cried aloud for vengeance from her chaste gridiron; and only a brave woman's taste, time, and temper were sacrificed on that domestic altar.

The vexed question of light was settled by buying a quantity of bayberry wax for candles; and, on discovering that no one knew how to make them, pine knots were introduced, to be used when absolutely necessary. Being summer, the evenings were not long, and the weary fraternity found it no great hardship to retire with the birds. The inner light was sufficient for most of them. But Mrs. Lamb rebelled. Evening was the only time she had to herself, and while the tired feet rested the skilful hands mended torn frocks and little stockings, or anxious heart forgot its burden in a book.

So "mother's lamp" burned steadily, while the philosophers built a new heaven and earth by moonlight; and through all the metaphysical mists and philanthropic pyrotechnics of that period Sister Hope played her own little game of "throwing light," and none but the moths were the worse for it.

Such farming probably was never seen before since Adam delved. The band of brothers began by spading garden and field; but a few days of it lessened their ardor amazingly. Blistered hands and aching backs suggested the expediency of permitting the use of cattle till the workers were better fitted for noble toil by a summer of the new life.

Brother Moses brought a yoke of oxen from his farm, — at least, the philosophers thought so till it was discovered that one of the animals was a cow; and Moses confessed that he "must be let down easy, for he couldn't live on garden sarse entirely."

Great was Dictator Lion's indignation at this lapse from virtue. But time pressed, the work must be done; so the meek cow was permitted to wear the yoke and the recreant brother continued to enjoy forbidden draughts in the bam, which dark proceeding caused the children to regard him as one set apart for destruction.

The sowing was equally peculiar, for, owing to some mistake, the three brethren, who devoted themselves to this graceful task, found when about half through the job that each had been sowing a different sort of grain in the same field; a mistake which caused much perplexity, as it could not be remedied; but, after a long consultation and a good deal of laughter, it was decided to say nothing and see what would come of it.

The garden was planted with a generous supply of useful roots and herbs; but, as manure was not allowed to profane the virgin soil, few of these vegetable treasures ever came up. Purslane reigned supreme, and the disappointed planters ate it philosophically, deciding that Nature knew what was best for them, and would generously supply their needs, if they could only learn to digest her "sallets" and wild roots.

The orchard was laid out, a little grafting done, new trees and vines set, regardless of the unfit season and entire ignorance of the husbandmen, who honestly believed that in the autumn they would reap a bounteous harvest.

Slowly things got into order, and rapidly rumors of the new experiment went abroad, causing many strange spirits to flock thither, for in those days communities were the fashion and transcendentalism raged wildly. Some came to look on and laugh, some to be supported in poetic idleness, a few to believe sincerely and work heartily. Each member was allowed to mount his favorite hobby and ride it to his heart's content. Very queer were some of the riders, and very rampant some of the hobbies.

One youth, believing that language was of little consequence if the spirit was only right, startled new-comers by blandly greeting them with "Good-morning, damn you," and other remarks of an equally mixed order. A second irrepressible being held that all the emotions of the soul should be freely expressed, and illustrated his theory by antics that would have sent him to a lunatic asylum, if, as an unregenerate wag said, he had not already been in one. When his spirit soared, he climbed trees and shouted; when doubt assailed him, he lay upon the floor and groaned lamentably. At joyful periods, he raced, leaped, and sang; when sad, he wept aloud; and when a great thought burst upon him in the watches of the night, he crowed like a jocund cockerel, to the great delight of the children and the great annoyance of the elders. One musical brother fiddled whenever so moved, sang sentimentally to the four little girls, and put a music-box on the wall when he hoed corn.

Brother Pease ground away at his uncooked food, or browsed over the farm on sorrel, mint, green fruit, and new vegetables. Occasionally he took his walks abroad, airily attired in an unbleached cotton poncho, which was the nearest approach to the primeval costume he was allowed to indulge in. At midsummer he retired to the wilderness, to try his plan where the woodchucks were without prejudices and huckleberry-bushes were hospitably full. A sunstroke unfortunately spoilt his plan, and he returned to semi-civilization a sadder and wiser man.

Forest Absalom preserved his Pythagorean silence, cultivated his fine dark lodes, and worked like a beaver, setting an excellent example of brotherly love, justice, and fidelity by his upright life. He it was who helped overworked Sister Hope with her heavy washes, kneaded the endless succession of batches of bread, watched over the children, and did the many tasks left undone by the brethren, who were so busy discussing and defining great duties that they forgot to perform the small ones.

Moses White placidly plodded about, "chorin' raound," as he called it, looking like an old-time patriarch, with his silver hair and flowing beard, and saving the community from many a mishap by his thrift and Yankee shrewdness.

Brother Lion domineered over the whole concern; for, having put the most money into the speculation, he was resolved to make it pay, — as if anything founded on an ideal basis could be expected to do so by any but enthusiasts.

Abel Lamb simply revelled in the Newness, firmly believing that his dream was to be beautifully realized and in time not only little Fruitlands, but the whole earth, be turned into a Happy Valley. He worked with every muscle of his body, for *he* was in deadly earnest. He taught with his whole head and heart; planned and sacrificed, preached and prophesied, with a soul full of the purest aspirations, most unselfish purposes, and desires for a life devoted to God and man, too high and tender to bear the rough usage of this world.

It was a little remarkable that only one woman ever joined this community. Mrs. Lamb merely followed wheresoever her husband led, — "as ballast for his balloon," as she said, in her bright way.

Miss Jane Gage was a stout lady of mature years, sentimental, amiable, and lazy. She wrote verses copiously, and had vague yearnings and graspings after the unknown, which led her to believe herself fitted for a higher sphere than any she had yet adorned.

Having been a teacher, she was set to instructing the children in the common branches. Each adult member took a turn at the infants; and, as each taught in his own way, the result was a chronic state of chaos in the minds of these much-afflicted innocents.

Sleep, food, and poetic musings were the desires of dear Jane's life, and she shirked all duties as clogs upon her spirit's wings. Any thought of lending a hand with the domestic drudgery never occurred to her; and when to the question, "Are there any beasts of burden on the place?" Mrs. Lamb answered, with a face that told its own tale, "Only one woman!" the buxom Jane took no shame to herself, but laughed at the joke, and let the stout-hearted sister tug on alone.

Unfortunately, the poor lady hankered after the flesh-pots, and endeavored to stay herself with private sips of milk, crackers, and cheese, and on one dire occasion she partook of fish at a neighbor's table.

One of the children reported this sad lapse from virtue, and poor Jane was publicly reprimanded by Timon.

"I only took a little bit of the tail," sobbed the penitent poetess.

"Yes, but the whole fish had to be tortured and slain that you might tempt your carnal appetite with that one taste of the tail. Know ye not, consumers of flesh meat, that ye are nourishing the wolf and tiger in your bosoms?"

At this awful question and the peal of laughter which arose from some of the younger brethren, tickled by the ludicrous contrast between the stout sinner, the stem judge, and the naughty satisfaction of the young detective, poor Jane fled from the room to pack her trunk and return to a world where fishes" tails were not forbidden fruit.

Transcendental wild oats were sown broadcast that year, and the fame thereof has not yet ceased in the land; for, futile as this crop seemed to outsiders, it bore an invisible harvest, worth much to those who planted in earnest. As none of the members of this particular community have ever recounted their experiences before, a few of them may not be amiss, since the interest in these attempts has never died out and Fruitlands was the most ideal of all these castles in Spain.

A new dress was invented, since cotton, silk, and wool were forbidden as the product of slave-labor, worm-slaughter, and sheep-robbery. Tunics and trowsers of brown linen were the only wear. The women's skirts were longer, and their straw hat-brims wider than the men's, and this was the only difference. Some persecution lent a charm to the costume, and the long-haired, linen-clad reformers quite enjoyed the mild martyrdom they endured when they left home.

Money was abjured, as the root of all evil. The produce of the land was to supply most of their wants, or be exchanged for the few things they could not grow. This idea had its inconveniences; but self-denial was the fashion, and it was surprising how many things one can do without.

When they desired to travel, they walked, if possible, begged the loan of a vehicle, or boldly entered car or coach, and, stating their principles to the officials, took the consequences. Usually their dress, their earnest frankness, and gentle resolution won them a passage; but now and then they met with hard usage, and had the satisfaction of suffering for their principles.

On one of these penniless pilgrimages they took passage on a boat, and, when fare was demanded, artlessly offered to talk, instead of pay. As the boat was well under way and they actually had not a cent, there was no help for it. So Brothers Lion and Lamb held forth to the assembled passengers in their most eloquent style. There must have been something effective in this conversation, for the listeners were moved to take up a contribution for these inspired lunatics, who preached peace on earth and good-will to man so earnestly, with empty pockets. A goodly sum was collected; but when the captain presented it the reformers proved that they were consistent even in their madness, for not a penny would they accept, saying, with a look at the group about them, whose indifference or contempt had changed to interest and respect, "You see how I well we get on without money"; and so went I serenely on their way, with their linen blouses flapping airily in the cold October wind.

They preached vegetarianism everywhere and resisted all temptations of the flesh, contentedly eating apples and bread at well-spread tables, and much afflicting hospitable hostesses by denouncing their food and taking away their appetites, discussing the "horrors of shambles," the "incorporation of the brute in man," and "on elegant abstinence the sign of a pure soul." But, when the perplexed or offended ladies asked what they should eat, they got in reply a bill of fare consisting of "bowls of sunrise for breakfast," "solar seeds of the sphere," "dishes from Plutarch's chaste table," and other viands equally hard to find in any modem market.

Reform conventions of all sorts were haunted by these brethren, who said many wise things and did many foolish ones. Unfortunately, these wanderings interfered with their harvest at home; but the rule was to do what the spirit moved, so they left their crops to Providence and went a-reaping in wider and, let us hope, more fruitful fields than their own.

Luckily, the earthly providence who watched over Abel Lamb was at hand to glean the scanty crop yielded by the "uncorrupted land," which, "consecrated to human freedom," had received "the sober culture of devout men."

About the time the grain was ready to house, some call of the Oversoul wafted all the men away. An easterly storm was coming up and the yellow stacks were sure to be ruined. Then Sister Hope gathered her forces. Three little girls, one boy (Timon's son), and herself, harnessed to clothes-baskets and Russia-linen sheets, were the only teams she could command; but with these poor appliances the indomitable woman got in the grain and saved food for her young, with the instinct and energy of a mother-bird with a brood of hungry nestlings to feed.

This attempt at regeneration had its tragic as well as comic side, though the world only saw the former.

With the first frosts, the butterflies, who had sunned themselves in the new light through the summer, took flight, leaving the few bees to see what honey they had stored for winter use. Precious little appeared beyond the satisfaction of a few months of holy living.

At first it seemed as if a chance to try holy dying also was to be offered them. Timon, much disgusted with the failure of the scheme, decided to retire to the Shakers, who seemed to be the only successful community going.

"What is to become of us?" asked Mrs. Hope, for Abel was heart-broken at the bursting of his lovely bubble.

"You can stay here, if you like, till a tenant is found. No more wood must be cut, however, and no more corn ground. All I have must be sold to pay the debts of the concern, as the responsibility rests with me," was the cheering reply.

"Who is to pay us for what we have lost? I gave all I had, — furniture, time, strength, six months of my children's lives, — and all are wasted. Abel gave himself body and soul, and is almost wrecked by hard work and disappointment. Are we to have no return for this, but leave to starve and freeze in an old house, with winter at hand, no money, and. hardly a friend left; for this wild scheme has alienated nearly all we had. You talk much about justice. Let us have a little, since there is nothing else left."

But the woman's appeal met with no reply but the old one: "It was an experiment. We all risked something, and must bear our losses as we can."

With this cold comfort, Timon departed with his son, and was absorbed into the Shaker brotherhood, where he soon found that the order of things was reversed, and it was all work and no play.

Then the tragedy began for the forsaken little family. Desolation and despair fell upon Abel. As his wife said, his new beliefs had alienated many friends. Some thought him mad, some unprincipled. Even the most kindly thought him a visionary, whom it was useless to help till he took more practical views of life. All stood aloof, saying: "Let him work out his own ideas, and see what they are worth."

He had tried, but it was a failure. The world was not ready for Utopia yet, and those who attempted to found it only got laughed at for their pains. In other days, men could sell all and give to the poor, lead lives devoted to holiness and high thought, and, after the persecution was over, find themselves honored as saints or martyrs. But in modem times these things are out of fashion. To live for one's principles, at all costs, is a dangerous speculation; and the failure of an ideal, no matter how humane and noble, is harder for the world to forgive and forget than bank robbery or the grand swindles of corrupt politicians.

Deep waters now for Abel, and for a time there seemed no passage through. Strength and spirits were exhausted by hard work and too much thought. Courage failed when, looking about for help, he saw no sympathizing face, no hand outstretched to help him, no voice to say cheerily,

"We all make mistakes, and it takes many experiences to shape a life. Try again, and let us help you."

Every door was closed, every eye averted, every heart cold, and no way open whereby he might earn bread for his children. His principles would not permit him to do many things that others did; and in the few fields where conscience would allow him to work, who would employ a man who had flown in the face of society, as he had done?

Then this dreamer, whose dream was the life of his life, resolved to carry out his idea to the bitter end. There seemed no place for him here, — no work, no friend. To go begging conditions was as ignoble as to go begging money. Better perish of want than sell one's soul for the sustenance of his body. Silently he lay down upon his bed, turned his face to the wall, and waited with pathetic patience for death to cut the knot which he could not untie. Days and nights went by, and neither food nor water passed his lips. Soul and body were dumbly struggling together, and no word of complaint betrayed what either suffered.

His wife, when tears and prayers were unavailing, sat down to wait the end with a mysterious awe and submission; for in this entire resignation of all things there was an eloquent significance to her who knew him as no other human being did.

"Leave all to God," was his belief; and in this crisis the loving soul clung to this faith, sure that the Allwise Father would not desert this child who tried to live so near to Him. Gathering her children about her, she waited the issue of the tragedy that was being enacted in that solitary room, while the first snow fell outside, untrodden by the footprints of a single friend.

But the strong angels who sustain and teach perplexed and troubled souls came and went, leaving no trace without, but working miracles within. For, when all other sentiments had faded into dimness, all other hopes died utterly; when the bitterness of death was nearly over, when body was past any pang of hunger or thirst, and soul stood ready to depart, the love that outlives all else refused to die. Head had bowed to defeat, hand had grown weary with too heavy tasks, but heart could not grow cold to those who lived in its tender depths, even when death touched it.

Orchard House at Concord, Massachusetts
The Alcott home of later years

"My faithful wife, my little girls, — they have not forsaken me, they are mine by ties that none can break. What right have I to leave them alone?

What right to escape from the burden and the sorrow I have helped to bring? This duty remains to me, and I must do it manfully. For their sakes, the world will forgive me in time; for their sakes, God will sustain me now."

Too feeble to rise, Abel groped for the food that always lay within his reach, and in the darkness and solitude of that memorable night ate and drank what was to him the bread and wine of a new communion, a new dedication of heart and life to the duties that were left him when the dreams fled.

In the early dawn, when that sad wife crept fearfully to see what change had come to the patient face on the pillow, she found it smiling at her, saw a wasted hand outstretched to her, and heard a feeble voice cry bravely, "Hope!"

What passed in that little room is not to be recorded except in the hearts of those who suffered and endured much for love's sake. Enough for us to know that soon the wan shadow of a man came forth, leaning on the arm that never failed him, to be welcomed and cherished by the children, who never forgot the experiences of that time.

"Hope" was the watchword now; and, while the last logs blazed on the hearth, the last bread and apples covered the table, the new commander, with recovered courage, said to her husband, —

"Leave all to God — and me. He has done his part, now I will do mine."

"But we have no money, dear."

"Yes, we have. I sold all we could spare, and have enough to take us away from this snowbank."

"Where can we go?"

"I have engaged four rooms at our good neighbor, Lovejoy's. There we can live cheaply till spring. Then for new plans and a home of our own, please God."

"But, Hope, your little store won't last long, and we have no friends."

"I can sew and you can chop wood. Lovejoy offers you the same pay as he gives his other men; my old friend, Mrs. Truman, will send me all the work I want; and my blessed brother stands by us to the end. Cheer up, dear heart, for while there is work and love in the world we shall not suffer."

"And while I have my good angel Hope, I shall not despair, even if I wait another thirty years before I step beyond the circle of the sacred little world in which I still have a place to fill."

So one bleak December day, with their few possessions piled on an ox-sled, the rosy children perched atop, and the parents trudging arm in arm behind, the exiles left their Eden and faced the world again.

"Ah, me! my happy dream. How much I leave behind that never can be mine again," said Abel, looking back at the lost Paradise, lying white and chill in its shroud of snow.

"Yes, dear; but how much we bring away," answered brave-hearted Hope, glancing from husband to children.

"Poor Fruitlands! The name was as great a failure as the rest!" continued Abel, with a sigh, as a frostbitten apple fell from a leafless bough at his feet.

But the sigh changed to a smile as his wife added, in a half-tender, half-satirical tone, —

"Don't you think Apple Slump would be a better name for it, dear?"

[After so many years Louisa Alcott very naturally forgot a few unimportant details when she wrote "Transcendental Wild Oats," yet they are important enough to set straight. Papers lately found show the exit from Fruitlands to have taken place in January. She also speaks of stoves in the old house. This is a mistake. The old chimney was taken down by Joseph Palmer's grandson, Mr. Alvin Holman, many years after the Fruitlands Community was broken up.]

Appendix

Catalogue of the Original Fruitlands Library

Hexapla; the Greek text of the New Testament with six English Versions in parallel columns. 4to. London. 1840.

Confucii Sinarum Philosophus. Folio. 1787.

The Laws of Menu. Translated by Sir William Jones.

The Desatir; Sacred Writings of the Ancient Persian Prophets. Persian and English. Bombay. 1818.

The Divine Pymander of Hermes Trismegistus. London. 1650.

Juliana's Revelation of Divine Love. 1670.

St. Bridget's Revelations. Nuremberg. 1500.

Behmen's Works. Theosophia Revelata, das ist alle Gottliche Schriften des Jacob Behmens. With Life, etc., edited by J. G. Gechtels. I vol., folio. 4,500 pages. 1715.

- The Rev. William Law's edition, containing the Aurora or Morning Red; the Three Principles; Man's Threefold Life; Answer to the Forty Questions concerning the Soul; Signatura Rerum; The Four Complexions; The Mysterium Magnum, etc. 4 vols. 4to. London. 1764.

- Signatura Rerum; Supersensual Life, etc, 4to. London. 1781.

- Way to Christ. London. 1775.

- Teutonic Philosophy. London. 1770.

- Life, by Francis Okely. Northampton. 1780.

- Theosophick Philosophy Unfolded, by Edward Taylor. London. 1691.

Behmen's Works. Epistles and Apologies, by John Sparrow. London. 1662.

Graber and Gichtel. Kurze Eroffnnug und Unweisung der dreyen Pincipien und Welten in Menschen. Berlin. 1779.

H. Jansen. A Spiritual Journey. 4to. London. 1659.

Lamy. La Vie de St. Bernard. 4to. Paris. 1648.

Henrico Khurrath. Amphitheatrum Sapientiae Aeternae. Folio. Magdeburg. 1602.

Molinos' Spiritual Guide. Dublin. 1798.

S. Pordage. Mundorum Explicatio. London. 1663.

J. Pordage. Theologia Mystica. London. 1683.

De Sales' Introduction to a Devout Life. London. 1686.

Matthew Weyer's Narrow Path of Divine Truth. London. 1683.

Important Truths relating to Spiritual and Practical Christianity. London. 1769.

Unpremeditated Thoughts of God.

H. Hugonis Pia Desideria. London. 1677.

Theologiae Pacificae itemque Mysticae. Amstelodami. 1622.
Immanuel. By S. S. London. 1669.
A. Bourignon. Light in Darkness. London. 1703.
- Solid Virtue. London. 1699.
- Life and Sentiments. London. 1699.
- Light of the World. London. 1696,
Madame Guyon. Poesies et Cantiques Spirituels. Cologne. 1722.
Madame Guyon. Life by Brooke. Bristol. 1806.
- Lettres Chrétiennes, etc. 5 vols. London. 1767.
- Les Opuscules Spirituels. 2 vols. Paris. 1790.
- Life. 3 vols. Paris. 1791.
- Polemics. London. 1841.
- Selections in German. Manheim. 1787.
Fénelon's Dissertation on Pure Love. London. 1750.
- Account of Madame Guyon. London. 1759.
Fenelon's Justifications de Madame Guyon. Paris. 1790.
- Maxims of the Saints. London. 1698.
- Dialogues of the Dead. 2 vols. Berwick. 1770.
- Lives and Maxims of Ancient Philosophers.
London. 1726.
Thomas à Kempis. Imitation of Christ. By Dr. Stanhope. London. 1759.
William Law. Way to Divine Knowledge
- Spirit of Prayer.
- Spirit of Love.
- Christian Perfection.
- Serious Call.
- Letters.
- Appeal.
- Answer to Dr. Trapp.
- Case of Reason.
- Remarks on the Fable of the Bees, i vol.
- Tracts.
- Christian's Manual (extracts).
- Reply to the Bishop of Bangor on the Sacrament. 1719.
- Spiritual Fragments (extracts).
- Jordani Brunonis Opera. Paris. 1654.
Swedenborg. Arcana Coelestia.
- Heavenly Doctrine. Cambridge. 1820.
- Heaven and Hell. London. 1823.
Coleridge. Biographia Literaria. 2 vols. N. York. 1817.
- Aids to Reflection. Burlington. 1829.
- Friend. Burlington. 1831.
Graeve's Manuscripts. 12 vols. 4to. 1828 to 1842.
- Maxims. London. 1826.

Novalis Schriften. Berlin. 1836.
Lane's Third Dispensation. London. 1841.
Alcott's Conversations with Children on the Gospels. 2 vols. Boston. 1836.
- Record of a School. Boston. 1835.
Krummacher's Parabeln. 2 vols. Essen. 1840.
Spinoza's Works and Epistles. 4to. 1777.
Malebranche's Search after Truth. 2 vols. London. 1695.
- Christian Conferences. London. 1695.
Wilmott's Lives of the Sacred Poets. London. 1834.
G. Herbert's Poems. London. 1835.
R. Crashaw's Steps to the Temple. London. 1670.
Thomas Fletcher's Purple Island. London. 1783.
Giles Fletcher's Christ's Victory. London. 1783.
Quarles's Emblems and Hieroglyphics. London. 1680.
- Divine Fancies. London. 1680.
Huarte's Wits Commonwealth, or Politeuphuia. London. 1598.
Southcott's Tracts.
Dr. A. Bury's Naked Gospel. 4to. London. 1691.
Bromley's Sabbath of Rest, etc. London. 1761.
Robert Barclay's Apology. London. 1765.
N. Robinson's Christian Philosopher. London. 1758.
Poiret. On the Restoration of Man. London. 1713.
- Divine Economy. London. 1713.
Virgin in Eden. London. 1741.
Rev. R. Clarke. Gospel of the Daily Service. London. 1767.
- Jesus the Nazarene. London. 1770.
- Spiritual Voice. London. 1700.
Tracts. By Jane Lead.
Boehms' History of Pietism. London. 1707.
Franck. Pietas Hallensis. London. 1705.
Pascal's Thoughts on Religion. London. 1806.
P. Buchius on the Divine Being. London. 1693.
Bellarmine's Soul's Ascension to God. London. 1703.
R. Wilkinson's Saint's Travel to Canaan. London. 1650.
Man before Adam. London. 1656.
T, Hartley's Paradise Restored. London. 1764.
J. Serjeant's Transnatural Philosophy. London. 1700.
Henry More. Platonic. Cambridge. 1642.
- Works. Folio. London. 1642.
Universal Restitution. London. 1761.
Peter Sterry on the Freedome of the Will. Folio. London. 1675.
Pathomachia, or the Battell of Affections shadowed by a faigned siedge of the Citie Pathopolis. 4to. London. 1631.
L. Howell's Desiderius, or the Original Pilgrim. London. 1716.

Bernard's Isle of Man. London. 1803.
Olbia, or the New Island. 4to. London. 1600.
Ramsey's Philosophical Principles of Natural and Revealed Religion. Glasgow. 2 vols. 4to. 1748.
Justus Lipsius. On Constancy. London. 1654.
General Delusion of Christians. London. 1714.
Norris. On Love. London. 1723.
- Amoris Effigies, of Waring. London. 1744.
- On Matrimony. 2 vols. London. 1739.
- Ideal World. 2 vols. London. 1701.
Wither's Britain's Remembrancer. London. 1628.
Dr. Bryom's Miscellaneous Poems. 2 vols. Manchester. 1773.
Du Bartas' Divine Weekes and Workes. By Josiah Sylvester. 670 pages. Folio. London. 1641.
Verstegan's Restitution of Decayed Intelligence. 4to. London.
Rei Rusticae Auctores Latini Veteres. M. Cato, L. Columella, M. Varo. Palladius. 1595.
Tusser's Husbandry. London. 1744.
Evelyn. Kalendarium Hortense. London. 1699.
Porphyry on Abstinence from Animal Food, By T. Taylor. London. 1823.
Tyron. Averroeana, or Letters from Averroes. London. 1687.
Tyron. Way to Health. London. 1697.
- Knowledge of Man's Self. London. 1703.
- Letters, Philosophical, Theological, and Moral. London. 1700.
- Self-Knowledge. London. 1703.
- On Dreams. London. 1691.
Newton's Return to Nature. London. 1811.
Sir J. Floyer's Ψυχρολουσία. London. 1732,
R. T. Claridge's Hydropathy. London. 1842.
J. H. Cohausen. Hermippus Redivivus. London. 1771.
Thomas Stanley's History of Philosophy. 750 pages. Folio. London. 1700.
Iamblichus on the Mysteries. Translated by T. Taylor.
- Life of Pythagoras. By T. Taylor.
Dacier's Lives of Pythagoras and Hierocles. London. 1707.
Plato's Works, containing with the fifty-five Dialogues and twelve Epistles the substance of nearly all the existing Greek MSS. Commentaries and scholia on Plato. By Thomas Taylor. 5 vols. 4to. London. 1804.
Plotinus. Select Works. By T. Taylor. London. 1817.
- On Suicide. By T. Taylor. London. 1834.
Proclus. Commentaries on Euclid, by T. Taylor. 2 vols. 4to. London. 1788.
- Six Books on Plato's Theology. By T. Taylor. 2 vols. 4to. London. 1816.
- Commentaries on the Timaeus of Plato. By T, Taylor. 2 vols. 4to. London. 1820.
- Fragments. By T. Taylor. London. 1825.

- Ten Doubts, etc. London. 1833.
Stanhope's Epictetus. London. 1721.
Xenophon's Banquet. By Dr. Wei wood. London. 1710.
Dr. J. Welwood's Essay on Socrates. London. 1710.
Xenophon's Memoirs of Socrates. By Sarah Fielding. London. 1788.
Plutarch's Morals. 5 vols. London. 1694.
- Lives. By Langhorn. 8 vols. London. 1821.
Seneca's Morals. London. 1688.
Marcus Antonius. London. 1534.
Julii Pacii a Berega in Porphyii Isagogen et Aristotelis Organum. 4to. Geneva. 1605.
Aristotle's Metaphysics. By T. Taylor. 4to. London. 1801.
- 4to. Greek and Latin. (Jul. Pacius.) Geneva. 1605.
- Greek and Latin (Jul. Pacius.)
Thomas Taylor. Dissertation on the Philosophy of Aristotle. 4to. London. 1812.
- Theoretic Arithmetic. 1816.
- Select Works of Porphyry. London. 1823.
- Orcellus Lucanus, etc. London. 1831.
- See Proclus, Plato, etc.
William Bridgman. On the Nicomachean Ethics of Aristotle; with Greaves's MS. Notes. 4to. London. 1807.
- Translations of Greek Moralists. 1804.
Burton's Anatomy of Melancholy. 8vo. 743 pp. London. 1838.
Bacon. Novum Organum. Amstelodami. 1660.
- Wisdom of the Ancients. London. 1836.
Sir T. Browne. Religio Medici, and Urn Burial. London.
J. Moerman. Apologia Creaturum and other Emblems. 4to. 1584.
Redelium. Apophthegmata Symbolica.
- Annus Symbolicus. 4to.
Menestrerii Philosophia Imaginum. Amstelodami. 1695.
Alciati Emblemata, cum Claudii Minois Commentariis Raphelengii. 1608.
Muncherus, Mythographi Latini. Amstelodami, 1681.
Astrey's Emblems. 2 vols. London. 1700.
Choice Emblems, Divine and Moral. London. 1732.
Dr. F. Lee's Ἀπολειπόμενα, or Theological, Mathematical, and Physical Dissertations. 2 vols. London. 1752.
Dr. Godwin. Synopsis Antiquitatum Hebraicarum. 4to. London. 1690.
Walter Whiter. Etymologicum Magnum. 4to. Cambridge. 1800.
B. Holloway's Physical and Theological Originals. Oxford. 1751.
Jablonskii. Pantheon Aegyptiorum. 2 vols. Francofurti. 1750.
Homberg. Mythologie der Griechen und Romer. Leipzig. 1839.
Pinnock's Iconology.

Aesop's Fables and other eminent Mythologists, by L'Estrange. 480 pp., folio. London. 1692.

- Greek and Latin. Trajecti ad Rhenam. 1689.

Hesiod's Works. By T. Cooke. London. 1740.

Pindari. Alcoei, Sapphus, Stesichori, Anacreontis, Simonidis, Alcmonis, etc. Graece et Latine. Heidelberge. 1597.

Wintertoni. Poetae Minores Graeci. Graece et Latine. Cantabrigiae. 1677.

Hippocrates. By Sprengell. London. 1708.

Van Helmont, Oriatrike, or Physic Refined. 1200 pp. Folio. London. 1662.

- Treatise on Natural Philosophy. London. 1687.

- Paradoxical Discourses. London. 1685.

Paracelsus. Archidoxis. London. 1663.

Roger Bacon. Opus Magnus.

- Mirror of Alchymy. 1597.

- Admirable Force of Nature and Art.

Pyrotechny Asserted and Illustrated. London. 1658.

Reginald Scot's Discovery of Witchcraft. Folio. London. 1665.

E. Sibley's Key to Physic and Occult Sciences. 4to. London.

Magiae Adamiae, or the Antiquitie of Magic. London. 1650.

Centrum Naturae Concentratum, or the Salt of Nature Regenerated. London. 1696.

Stilling's Theory of Pneumatology. London. 1834.

J. C. Colquhoun. Isis Revelata. 2 vols. Edinburgh. 1836.

K. Digbey. On the Nature of Bodies; and Man's Soule. 4to. London. 1645.

The Vital Principle, or Physiology of Man. London. 1838.

Green's Vital Dynamics. London. 1838.

William Cooper's Jehior, or Day of Dawning, Golden Ass, and Catalogue of Mystic Books. London. 1673.

H. C. Agrippa. Occult Philosophy. 4to. London. 1655.

- Vanity of the Arts and Sciences.

www.ingramcontent.com/pod-product-compliance
Lightning Source LLC
Chambersburg PA
CBHW032018040426
42448CB00006B/653